D0219104

NCLUSION in the
EARLY YEARS

Education at SAGE

SAGE is a leading international publisher of journals, books, and electronic media for academic, educational, and professional markets.

Our education publishing includes:

- accessible and comprehensive texts for aspiring education professionals and practitioners looking to further their careers through continuing professional development

- inspirational advice and guidance for the classroom

- authoritative state of the art reference from the leading authors in the field

Find out more at: **www.sagepub.co.uk/education**

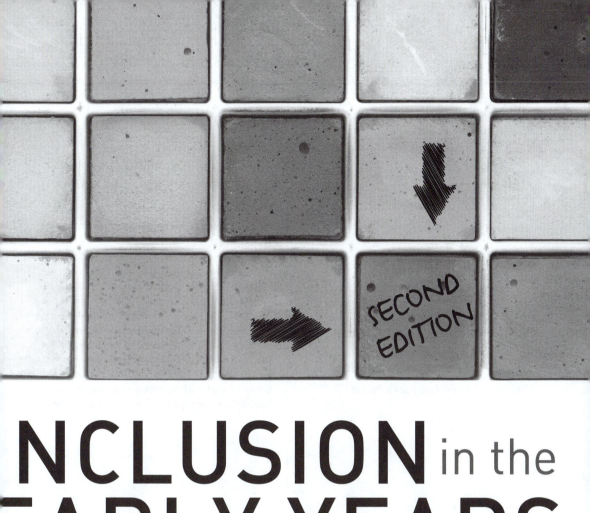

SECOND EDITION

NCLUSION in the EARLY YEARS

ATHY NUTBROWN AND **PETER CLOUGH**
with **FRANCES ATHERTON**

SAGE

Los Angeles | London | New Delhi
Singapore | Washington DC

Los Angeles | London | New Delhi
Singapore | Washington DC

SAGE Publications Ltd
1 Oliver's Yard
55 City Road
London EC1Y 1SP

SAGE Publications Inc.
2455 Teller Road
Thousand Oaks, California 91320

SAGE Publications India Pvt Ltd
B 1/I 1 Mohan Cooperative Industrial Area
Mathura Road
New Delhi 110 044

SAGE Publications Asia-Pacific Pte Ltd
3 Church Street
#10-04 Samsung Hub
Singapore 049483

Editor: Marianne Lagrange
Assistant editor: Kathryn Bromwich
Production editor: Nicola Marshall
Copyeditor: Sarah Bury
Proofreader: Jill Birch
Indexer: Author
Marketing manager: Catherine Slinn
Cover design: Wendy Scott
Typeset by: C&M Digitals (P) Ltd, Chennai, India
Printed in Great Britain by Ashford Colour Press Ltd

MIX
Paper from
responsible sources
FSC® C011748

© Cathy Nutbrown and Peter Clough with Frances
Atherton 2013

First edition published 2006
Reprinted 2008, 2010

Apart from any fair dealing for the purposes of
research or private study, or criticism or review, as
permitted under the Copyright, Designs and Patents
Act, 1988, this publication may be reproduced, stored
or transmitted in any form, or by any means, only with
the prior permission in writing of the publishers, or in
the case of reprographic reproduction, in accordance
with the terms of licences issued by the Copyright
Licensing Agency. Enquiries concerning reproduction
outside those terms should be sent to the publishers.

Library of Congress Control Number: 2012937731

British Library Cataloguing in Publication data

A catalogue record for this book is available from the
British Library

ISBN 978-1-4462-0322-4
ISBN 978-1-4462-0323-1 (pbk)

Professor Cathy Nutbrown is Head of the School of Education at the University of Sheffield, where she teaches and researches in the field of early childhood education.

Cathy began her career as a teacher of young children and has since worked in a range of settings and roles with children, parents, teachers, and other early childhood educators. Cathy is committed to finding ways of working 'with respect' with young children, and sees the concept of quality in the context of what it means to develop curriculum and pedagogy in the early years with the ambition of working in a climate of 'respectful education'.

She established the University of Sheffield MA in Early Childhood Education in 1998 and a Doctoral Programme in Early Childhood Education in 2008. In 2010 she contributed to the Tickell Review of the Early Years Foundation Stage. In June 2012 she reported on her year-long independent review for government on early years and childcare qualifications (The Nutbrown Review). She is Editor-in-Chief of the *Sage Journal of Early Childhood Research* and author of over fifty publications on aspects of early childhood education.

Professor Peter Clough is an Honorary Professor at the School of Education, University of Sheffield, where he teaches Masters and Doctoral students. Peter taught English and Drama in the 1970s, in London and later in a number of special schools. He has taught Inclusive Education and Early Childhood Education at the University of Sheffield, has been Professor of Inclusive Education at Queen's Belfast and at Liverpool Hope, and Research Fellow at the University of Chester.

Dr. Frances Atherton is Head of Higher Education Funding Council (HEFC) Programmes in the Faculty of Education and Children's Services at the University of Chester and Senior Lecturer in Early Years. She has a growing reputation in the early childhood field for her research on children under three and their learning through schemas. She teaches on a range of early childhood programmes, including BA Early Childhood Studies and MA Early Childhood. Frances also teaches research methodology and supervises undergraduate students, and those undertaking higher and research degrees.

Contents

List of tables

List of figures

List of boxes

Acknowledgements

This book includes reports from a study of European early childhood educators. The findings reported here benefited from the comments of delegates at a series of research conferences, including those of the British Educational Research Association and the European Early Childhood Education Research Association, as well as the Warwick International Early Childhood Education Research Conference, the Athens Institute for Educational Research Conference and the American Educational Research Association meeting. Referees from the *Journal of Early Childhood Research* and the *European Journal of Special Needs Education* provided useful critique. We are particularly pleased that Dr Frances Atherton has joined us in this second edition. Her contribution on policies in the four countries of the UK concludes each chapter.

We should like to thank: the practitioners from the UK, Denmark, Italy and Greece for their willing participation in the study which forms the basis of this book; colleagues at the University of Sheffield, Queen's University Belfast and the University of Chester; University of Sheffield Social Sciences Research Fund for initial funding to stimulate the project; Robin Taylor, Caron Carter, Debbie Critchley, Jools Page, Eve Cooke, Polly Dyer, 'Mary McVeigh', Jacqui Lloyd and Michael Kubiak for their contributions and critical feedback on the first edition. As ever, Marianne Lagrange, and the team at Sage have given us their unique publishing support throughout the project.

Cathy Nutbrown and Peter Clough

1

Politics and policies of inclusion

Introduction

Various claims are made about the success or failure of inclusion projects, for example Foucault's statement that:

> Realised through technologies that make visible particular objects of scrutiny ... inclusion functions as a panoptic mechanism through techniques which allow the assignment to each individual his 'true' name, his 'true' place, his 'true' body, his 'true' disease. (1977, p. 198)

Such accounts tend to be mostly descriptive and usually take for granted that the inclusive project is a transcendental 'good', a position which has been variously contested (Clough and Clough, 2013).

Throughout this book we examine assumptions and practices which bring to life some of the conceptual foundations of inclusive theory, policy and practice in the early years, focusing specifically on the years from birth to five. Inclusion is commonly an issue of *location*, by which we mean that there remains the view that as long as children share the same space, all are included. This, of course, is not the case, and many inclusive policies and projects do not meet with success because the necessary work on understanding and meeting individual needs is missing (or inadequate).

Graham and Slee (2008) point up the conflation of inclusion not only with location, but with a hegemonic centricity. 'Existing un-named in this tokenistic play that Said (1978, p. 310) calls the "pure politics of identity"', Graham and Slee (2008, p. 286) point out, are 'the characteristics held by dominant groups, which in Australia can be said to include whiteness, ablebodiedness and so on.'

A great deal happens – or doesn't – in the name of 'inclusion'. Graham and Slee identify 'a dangerous assumption' in the way in which different presumptions to include are 'concealed by the continued use of … generalised terms', and thus how inclusive education, which started life as a radical challenge to the traditions of schooling, becomes a means 'for explaining and protecting the status quo' (2008, p. 277). They remind us that 'to include is not necessarily to be inclusive. To shift pupils around on the educational chessboard is not in or of itself inclusive' (p. 278).

Policies can 'fail' because of 'uninterrogated normative assumptions that shape and drive policy' (Popkewitz and Lindblad, 2000), which result in no more than 'tinkering at the edges' and actually leaves things much as they were. For Harwood and Rasmussen (2002, p. 5) too, there is a need to arrest 'inclusion's need to speak of and identify otherness'.

In a brief history of the education of 'exceptional children' we can see three broad periods of educational policy (during the last 100 or so years), characterised by segregation, by integration and by inclusion. Children who were considered different from the 'normal' were either isolated at home with no access to provision of care and learning or they segregated schools and institutions, according to their impairments and difficulties. The critical histories of integration policies commonly identify a generalised global movement which in the context of its early days was surely a Good Thing: it sought to dismantle a gross distinction between students' abilities and their placement in either regular/'mainstream' or 'Special' schools; it sought to abolish the categorical silos into which individuals were sorted for such locational distribution; and in its tacit recognition of the importance of environment, it called for interventions in the first instance at the curricular, rather than the individual, level (Clough, 1999). But that set of policy developments barely disturbed the status quo of discriminatory social and educational provision, for the characteristic move is essentially from outer to inner, from margin to centre, from exceptional to normal, and so on. The early years have long been at the forefront of inclusive provision of education and care, inclusion (at least in terms of location) most often being the first and default option, with exclusion (to a specialised unit, centre or school) being an option once inclusion has failed.

And so the current phase of this brief history is a properly radical one: a broadly-understood *inclusion movement* which seeks to realise a sociology that insists that it is primarily in the environment where we will discover the root cause of, and the root solution to, exclusive practices. In contrast to *integration*, the inclusion ideology looks to change not the individual – so that s/he can be 'brought in from the cold' – but, quite simply, to change the environment, the school, society, the world. … It is no less radical a task. And in this sense it is about eradicating prejudice, injustice and inequality.

Many assumptions about what inclusion means, and looks like, go unchallenged, and make up, bind and constrain our social organisation. The task, then, is to enact inclusive policies in practice that challenge our preconceptions about human beings: children and their families, society, and success and failure themselves. If we can re-orientate our attention to the concept of inclusion (by challenging our own preconceptions), we can perhaps move from seeing inclusion as a set of practicalities to seeing it as an attitude of mind and will, for the practicalities of inclusion are merely imported remedies that 'compensate' for a 'normal' worldview. The wheel-chair ramp, for example, no more spells inclusion in itself than does anything else. Without picking apart our preconceptions, enmeshed as they are with our own take on the world, we can only appeal to practicalities of adjustment which 'fit' this worldview.

What we need to do, if we are to even approximate our goal as inclusion practitioners, is to engage in a personal interrogation of our own views and prejudices around difference and difficulty.

The propensity, across various policies, to measure inclusion in quantifiable, locational terms betrays our aspiration to 'de-centralise … normalcy'; we are just as much participants in centralised normalisation as we are critical proponents of de-centralisation. Sticking unswervingly to codified, quantitative measurements of inclusion does not necessarily equip us with the faculties of openness and critical reflection which allow us to challenge the norm of our societies.

Cultures, communities and curricula are by definition exclusive; we know things by their characteristics and by the boundaries of those features; we group things and we group people, for example, by religion, age, geography, role; we classify and we recognise what lies outside those classifications; were we unable to exclude we would be a different kind of being. Cultures, then, communities and curricula are as exclusive as they are inclusive.

Clough and Clough (2013) set out a series of simple theses which they identify as 'agnostic'. They are agnostic in the traditional sense of the term because they are properly sceptical of many current claims of the successes – and indeed 'failures' – of inclusive policies and projects. The theses are:

- Inclusion has an operational rather than conceptual focus. While we can give a dictionary definition of inclusion, what it is 'about' is such a relative, shifting, organic set of processes that any such characterisation will speak more of moral aspiration than empirics. In early education and care, we need to consider what happens in practice based on how we construct our own view of what it is to be inclusive.
- Inclusion is always in a 'state of becoming'. There can be no such thing as a fully inclusive, 'arrived-at' institution or society. In early

education and care, practitioners, families and children are constantly working in a state of 'becoming inclusive' for new challenges and new exclusionary factors can confront settings at any point. Thus:

- Inclusion can/must only be known by its outcomes – not by its rhetoric. There is a need for evidence, and an even greater need for agreement on what counts as evidence. As a set of statements, there is little to falsify inclusion, but there is a tendency to identify (and hence to measure) it in quantifiable, locational terms. In early education and care, it is the effects of successful inclusive practices and attitudes that really make a difference. But:

- There are as many versions of inclusion as there are people to be included – and as there are people who are to include them. So in early childhood education and care all practitioners, whatever their status, need to think through their own 'take' on what it is to be inclusive and how they adopt and enact inclusive policies and practices. Inclusion is not the exclusive property of any one domain, be that political, academic, professional, cultural or otherwise, and how it is defined differs uniquely from person to person. Each version is made up uniquely of a cultural confection of experiences, beliefs, ideologies, hopes, loves, disappointments, passions, fears, of hierarchies of tolerance, thresholds to our empathies and boundaries to our sympathies. And:

- Cultures, communities and curricula are, by definition, exclusive. We know things by their characteristics and by the boundaries of those features; we group things, we classify, and we recognise what lies outside those classifications; were we unable to exclude we should cease to be (as we know it). Therefore, cultures, communities, curricula, and indeed consciousness, are all as inalienably and dialectically exclusive as they are inclusive. In early education and care, where settings work with a diverse range of children and families who represent many heritages and backgrounds, values and beliefs, the creation of inclusive curricula is a key challenge. So:

- Inclusion must not be imposed from without, but developed in partnership with those who seek it. In early education and care ongoing professional support for all practitioners to work towards their own definitions and understandings of inclusion, and to work within a set of agreed inclusive practices is essential.

Because:

- Inclusion is ultimately about how people treat each other. (Such a claim takes us back to the first statement, and thus forms an endless loop.) And this, for us, is a matter of respect, and respectful educators, in so far as they can develop their professional knowledge and practice to be so, are inclusive.

Workshop 1 Seven statements about inclusion

Think through the seven statements put forward by Clough and Clough (2013):

1 Inclusion has an operational rather than conceptual focus.
2 Inclusion is always in a 'state of becoming'.
3 Inclusion can/must only be known by its outcomes – not its rhetoric.
4 There are as many versions of inclusion as there are people to be included.
5 Cultures, communities and curricula are, by definition, exclusive.
6 Inclusion must not be imposed from without.
7 Inclusion is ultimately about how people treat each other.

To what extent do these apply to you? Can you use them to identify your own attitudes and responses to inclusive issues as they affect you and your own practice, the children and families you work with, and your colleagues?

Throughout this book we shall continue to discuss issues which emanate from these ideas, and to identify inclusive issues and practices as they relate to young children, their families and their practitioners. Each of the subsequent chapters of this book ends with a related workshop which can be used by staff as part of their ongoing professional development, and some direct links to policy documents of England, Northern Ireland, Scotland and Wales.

Further reading 📖

Graham, L.J. and Slee, R. (2008) An illusory interiority: interrogating the discourse/s of inclusion. *Educational Philosophy and Theory*, 40(2): 277–93.

Popkewitz, T. and Lindblad, S. (2000) Educational governance and social inclusion and exclusion: some conceptual difficulties and problematics in policy and research. *Discourse: Studies in the Cultural Politics of Education*, 21(1): 5–44.

2

Cultures of inclusion in the early years

Introduction

There is a quite particular argument that informs the whole spirit and organisation of the book. The argument is quite simple: while their form may derive from specific and common policies, every early years setting represents a *culture* which is created by children, practitioners, parents and others. This is, in a sense, quite obvious, but we think it has important implications for how settings might be understood, developed and researched: much of the work which we report in this book is based on our systematic attempts as teachers and researchers to understand the meanings and stories at work in the lives of settings, their children, practitioners and parents. We believe that the book will not only add to the research community's understanding of early years policies and processes, but – and more importantly – help practitioners themselves to locate, reflect on and hence develop their own meanings and practices.

The book examines inclusion in its broadest senses (that is, concerning *all* children, parents and practitioners in *each and every* early years community) and seeks to demonstrate how inclusive processes can be embedded within early years curriculum, pedagogy and services which are designed to help all children reach their potential and achieve all that is possible for them.

One of the challenges in developing an *inclusive* agenda is finding a way to marry such with the agenda of *raising achievement*. Both are important: inclusion is an essential plank in the broad platform of social justice and raising achievement is a goal which all educators must hold for their pupils. *Raising achievement* has been presented within policy documents in terms of more narrowly-defined attainment and establishing standards and targets for all pupils, in England, from around five years old. Implicit within this normalising discourse is the categorising of individual children, whose (lower) attainment is attributed to factors such as ethnicity, gender, special educational needs and disability (SEND), family background or economic status.

Inclusion is a political and social struggle which foregrounds difference and identity and which involves whole setting and practitioner reform. It has moved from being specifically related to children with SEN to being a central part of global agenda. While special educators have come to understand inclusion as *both* increasing participation *and* removing exclusionary pressures, social inclusion, as it is framed within policy documents, problematises the social exclusion of disenfranchised groups and their disengagement from society (Sparkes, 1999). Social exclusion theories and policies are intended to avoid deficit models and pathologies (Leney, 1999), but they may contribute to the generation of a core of excluded groups and individuals.

The competing demands upon the wide range of early years practitioners in training, arising from the contrasting discourses and practices of *raising achievement* on the one hand and *inclusion* on the other, need to be reconciled in order to make it possible for the development of inclusive practices to be successful and for all children to reach their potential. Early childhood educators in training are expected to show some basic competencies in responding to young children's different abilities – whatever they might be. However, students' concerns about working with young children are often more focused on their own practice rather than children's enhanced achievement or inclusion. Thus early childhood educators in training may pathologise and problematise difference within their classrooms, especially with regard to young children's behaviour, in order to demonstrate their own competence in fulfilling the role for which they are training.

The individual child is constructed within the discourse of *raising achievement* and *promoting inclusion* in two polarised ways: either in relation to the norms of standards and targets or as outsiders 'in a society whose structural inequalities remain largely uninterrogated' (Levitas, 1998, p. 7). Thus, the individual practitioner is posited either as a technician within the *raising achievement* discourse – carrying out a series of steps in order to bring about particularly defined learning in the children they work with – or, in the context of *inclusion*, as undertaking institutional practices – following rules, procedures and routines, for example – which may present barriers to inclusion.

This book draws on reported research and presents findings from our own studies to describe attitudes and practices which can successfully address young children's learning needs in the context of *inclusive early years cultures*. So what do we mean when we speak of *inclusion* in this book? It is important to generate here a definition of inclusion that *works* – that is, that works throughout policies, practices and early years settings.

An operational definition of inclusion

The term 'inclusion' has been variously defined by many different writers and commentators but for the purposes of this book inclusion may be seen (following Booth, Ainscow and Kingston, 2006) as the *unified drive* towards maximal participation in and minimal exclusion from early years settings, from schools and from society. While there may appear to be some heterogeneity in the use of the term within governmental policy documents, any analysis must acknowledge a heterogeneity of meanings which reflect the development of inclusive early years and educational practices. Indeed, given that in practice 'inclusion' can only have an operational rather than conceptual meaning, it is clear that there are as many 'versions' of inclusion as there are early years settings – or, indeed, as individuals who make up those particular cultures of living and learning.

Social exclusion is an equally contestable and heterogeneous, though broader, construct concerned with non-participation in the economic, civic and social norms of society, and exclusion from school is among a number of factors which may contribute to lower educational attainment (Sparkes, 1999). For some parents of young children, their own social exclusion is manifest in such experiences as poor or temporary housing, unemployment, poverty, ill-health, lack of access to services, low levels of literacy and so on (Swadener et al., 2009). Levitas (1998) identified three separate discourses of social exclusion. These are:

- a *retributionist discourse*, which is concerned with poverty;
- a *moral underclass discourse*, which is centred on the moral and behavioural delinquency of the excluded;
- and a *social integrationist discourse*, which focuses on paid work.

These discourses differ markedly on how they specify boundaries, define people as insiders or outsiders and indicate how inclusion can be achieved. Levitas (1998) argues that social exclusion lacks analytical clarity, but its flexibility makes it a very powerful construct, while Barry (2002) suggested that the equally politically attractive term, social inclusion, diverts away from radical change and encourages compliance with the status quo.

However, these states of living are constructed or theorised. For many families, social exclusion means struggling in their lives with the range of difficulties outlined above and the exclusion of young children in a variety of ways. For these reasons, this book does not adopt a technical definition of inclusion/exclusion. We are also concerned about the effects of problematising difference by specifying potential groups 'at risk' of exclusion and in identifying particular *foci* of inclusion and exclusion. Nevertheless, we are interested in the similarities and differences in strategies for developing inclusive practices which are prompted by or targeted at particular groups. Throughout the book we examine examples of inclusion which highlight, for example, 'race' and gender, as well as disability or learning difficulty. Inter-disciplinary analyses across types of settings have enabled us to identify research studies and practices where new and radical approaches to inclusion are being developed.

So, in mapping the terrains of inclusion we are clear that potential arenas of inclusion and exclusion are extensive and far-reaching, affecting the lives of many children and their families. Some of these arenas are listed in Box 2.1.

Box 2.1   Arenas of inclusion/exclusion

Achievement
Age
Challenging behaviour
Disability
Disaffection
Emotional and behavioural difficulty
Employment
Gender
Housing
Language
Mental health
Obesity
Physical impairment
Poverty
Race/ethnicity
Religion
Sexual orientation
Social class
Special Educational Need

(Adapted from Clough, 1999)

(NB: This list is by no means exhaustive and readers will readily identify other categorical exclusions.)

Understanding difference

Understanding difference and how children think about difference is an important aspect of developing inclusive practices and policies and we should not forget how, at a very young age, children can develop political, social and cultural preferences which can, ultimately, lead to the generation of exclusionary values and behaviours (see, for example, Connolly, 2004).

Several studies have long established that issues of gender in children's play in the early years (Davies, 1989; Tarullo, 1994; MacNaughton, 1999) and gender identity is a strong feature in young children's lives (Connolly, 2004). Much has been written about 'sexual equality' and gender divides in society and interest in implications and effects of gender on young children's learning and experiences is rooted in a tradition of studies which have sought to understand, and later challenge, stereotypes and limited opportunities.

Tarullo (1994) suggested that girls and boys speak with 'different voices' in their experiences of the world and there is broad agreement in the literature spanning several decades that boys and girls show different kinds of behaviour and preferences in their play (Maccoby and Jacklin, 1974; Gussin Paley, 1984; McNaughton, 2000). Where girls and boys do share the same play area, they have often been found to use it differently, for example:

> The play area of playhouse is a largely female domain and children often assume stereotypical roles on entering it. Girls are pleased to act out stories and situations. However, boys seem unhappy in deferring to the girls in the context and I have often observed boys changing roles to become animals, introducing elements of aggression, noise and disruption to the situation. (D'Arcy, 1990, p. 84)

Clear preferences are often exhibited, perhaps because this is one way in which children create and begin to identify with their own gender. As MacNaughton suggests:

> Children's pretend play is rich in information about how they understand gender relations. As children play at 'having babies', 'being monsters', or 'making a hospital', children show others what they think girls and women can and should do, and what they think boys and men can and should do. (MacNaughton, 1999, p. 81)

Derman-Sparkes and the ABC Task Force suggest that:

> Between the ages of two and five years old, children are forming self-identities and building social interaction skills. At the same time, they are becoming aware of and curious about gender, race, ethnicity and disabilities. Gradually young children begin to figure out how they are alike and how they are different from other people, and how they feel about those differences. (1989, p. 43)

Limiting stereotypes can be challenged by clear strategies which involve:

- focusing on gender issues in practitioners' initial and post qualifying;
- recruiting men and women to work in settings;
- understanding the influence of families on children's constructions of gender;
- observing how children demonstrate what they know about men and women – and girls and boys – in their gendered play;
- remaining aware of the potentially limiting impact of gendered play on learning.

The following examples illustrate how gender plays out in early years settings and how intervention strategies might be employed to interrupt stereotypical behaviours.

Box 2.2   Homes and computers

The girls dominated the home corner area while the boys preferred the outside space and the computers. When questioned, the children said the home area was 'for girls' and the computers were 'for boys'. The teacher asked who did domestic chores at home and who used the family computer. The children's answers showed that stereotypical behaviour they displayed in the nursery was not reflecting their home lives, where some children saw women using computers and men washing up. Research has shown that young children often gravitate to stereotypical aspects of provision, often defying (or denying) the experience in their daily lives. The stereotypes were challenged through ongoing and deliberate intervention strategies which broadened out opportunities for children.

All-female staffs make it more difficult to model how women and men can work cooperatively, and use all aspects of provision. Male and female staff need to examine the messages they give to children about what men and women 'do' and demonstrate non-stereotypical behaviour.

Box 2.3   'Girls only' computer zone

The boys dominated the only computer for several sessions, not responding to practitioners' discussions about fairness, sharing and taking turns. The staff declared the computer area a 'girls only zone' until further notice. The boys, clearly shocked by the decision, complained about unfairness. Eventually, staff established a turn-taking system, reminding the boys how

(Continued)

(Continued)

they felt when they could not use the computer. This system was often successful when enforced by staff or when girls reported a breach of the rules.

Connolly (2004) argues that the lower educational performance of boys (particularly boys from families of lower socio-economic status) in the early years must be addressed by working in the 'Critical Gender Zone':

> ... the distance between what a child had already come to internalise in terms of their current experiences of gender relations and the degree to which they are able to reflect upon and deconstruct these with the help of others. (Connolly, 2004, pp. 229–30)

Box 2.4 Allowing boys into the home corner

In a project to allow boys more access to home-corner play, the children were first asked for their views. One 5-year-old girl said:

> The boys can't come in here [the house] 'cos they make a noise and they mess it up, and they act like dogs and angry husbands.

Another said:

> Sometimes I put the ironing board across the doorway so the boys can't get in ... 'cos there's no door and you need one.

As well as maintaining the usual home play space, staff encouraged children to suggest other role-play areas. Over the weeks they established a garage, a tropical fish shop, a hairdressing salon, a chip shop and an office, which gave rise to fewer instances of gender-dominated play and created spaces for boys to engage in more positive role-play activities which were not heavily dominated by the girls.

(Source: Nutbrown and Clough, 2009, pp. 201–2)

The role of parents and children's homes and families in influencing their 'out of setting' lives is an area which would benefit from further study. Though many studies have been developed on children's gendered identities, in the twenty-first-century context it is important fully to understand the impact of social and cultural influences on children's constructions of their gender identities. Three studies by teachers (Walters, 2002; Leslie, 2005; Tacey, 2005) examined the impact of families and parents on children's preferences for particular toys and of the construction of their gendered identities. Walters' (2002) study involving parents of ten 4-year-old children (five boys and five girls) showed that parents had clear ideas about the appropriateness of toys for girls and boys, and the boys liked cars, trucks and construction toys, while girls preferred soft toys, Barbie dolls and dressing-up games. Walters found a stereotypical view of girls' and boys' toys which led her to reflect on the implications for children's learning and all-round development. However, in a similar study, Tacey (2005) found that some parents were actively promoting non-stereotypical choices of toys at home and believed that the school promoted the development of narrow stereotypes of gendered identity.

Vivian Gussin Paley's work reminds us that combating stereotypical behaviours of young children is not easy:

> Kindergarten is a triumph of sexual stereotyping. No amount of adult subterfuge or propaganda deflects the five year old's passion for segregation by sex. They think they have invented the differences between boys and girls and, as with any new invention, must prove that it works. The doll corner is often the best place to collect evidence. It is not simply a place to play; it is a stronghold against ambiguity. (Gussin Paley, 1984, p. ix)

Practitioners need to be sensitive to children's emerging preferences so that all children benefit from a rich and broad range of learning experiences that are not limited by developing ideas of what is appropriate for girls or for boys. Girls may need support to extend beyond the home play and to take risks outdoors; and boys may need help to negotiate their way 'past the ironing board' to enjoy domestic play.

Difference is of interest to children, and the recognition of difference as positive rather than negative is an important aim for early childhood professionals. In a large-scale survey of a representative sample of 352 children aged 3 to 6 drawn from across Northern Ireland, Connolly et al. (2002) identified the detail of cultural and political awareness of young children. Four main levels of awareness were identified among the children:

1 Preference for particular cultural events and symbols.
2 Awareness of particular cultural events and symbols.
3 Tendency to identify with a particular community.
4 Tendency to make sectarian statements.

The authors consider the influences on young children's attitudes towards particular symbols of community and faith and identified three influential factors: family, local community and school. Of these, the nature of segregated schooling is a key influence in accounting for children's attitudes towards difference, with the majority (96%) of children attending Protestant or Catholic schools. Connolly et al. note:

> For any child, entering school for the first time represents a significant mile-stone in their lives. It is likely to be the first time that many will begin to interact with much larger numbers of other children and also to come under the influence of their older peers. When such environments are overwhelm-ingly Catholic or Protestant in their ethos, then it is not surprising to find that they can represent a fertile learning ground within which children's awareness about cultural and political events and symbols, as well as the attitudes and prejudices that often accompany these, increase rapidly. (2002, p. 37–38)

They identify the following implications for community relations work with young children which would promote more inclusive attitudes:

1 Children, from the age of 3, should be encouraged to explore and experience a range of different cultural practices, events and symbols and to appreciate and respect difference and cultural diversity.
2 From about the age of 5 onwards, children should be encouraged to understand the negative effects of sectarian stereotypes and preju-dices and to be able to identify them in their own attitudes, where appropriate.
3 For such strategies to be successful, nurseries and schools need to find ways of engaging and working closely with parents and the local community and, where appropriate, connecting with community relations and cultural diversity initiatives in the wider community.

Though Connolly et al. (2002) were working within a quite particular set of social, educational and political circumstances, they reached the conclusion that close working with parents and the local community and connecting with community relations and cultural diversity is an important maxim for all settings wherever they are located.

In the early years, some overarching factors can be seen to be of par-ticular importance. These are the issues of: 'rights'; curriculum; play; developmentally appropriate practice; and assessment. We want to devote the remainder of this chapter to a discussion of these issues and thus provide an underpinning for the book as a whole.

Children's rights and human rights

Issues of 'rights' are often central to a discussion of the education and care of young children with learning difficulties. However, decisions as to which rights best apply and in whose interests can often be complex. *Children's rights* and *human rights* have, for some time, been necessarily entangled, but that entanglement has led to confusion about the role of both the United Nations Convention on the Rights of the Child (UNESCO, 1992) and the European Convention on Human Rights (ECHR) (1994). In 1997, the intention of the UK government to incorporate the ECHR into UK domestic law was greeted with warnings that the UN Convention on the Rights of the Child should not be over-shadowed by the move towards human rights in general (Gunner, 1997). Lansdown (1998) saw the incorporation of the European Convention on Human Rights as:

> a step in the right direction. But for children, it is not enough. We must therefore welcome this commitment on the part of the government as progress towards the ultimate goal of societal recognition of children as holders of human rights. But we must also continue to argue for a commit-ment to full implementation of all the principles of the UN Convention of the Rights of the Child, in law, in policy and in practice. (p. 21)

As Phillips (2001) notes, practitioners in Reggio Emilia have ceased to talk of Special Educational Needs but have, instead, chosen to include discussion of Special Educational Rights in their dialogue about meeting young children's needs and access to curriculum. The UN Convention on the Rights of the Child is an important touchstone for early childhood practitioners. For example, Hyder's (2004) work with young refugee children is set in the context of the UN Convention on the Rights of the Child and she argues that play is a healing experience for young children affected by war and conflict. Hyder (2004) explores the importance of play for young refugee children's development. She considers the implications of war and conflict on young children and notes how opportunities for play are often denied them.

Such *rights* are only as useful as the actions they lead to, and so for children to have any *rights*, adults need to take on the necessary *respon-sibilities* to bring those rights into practical and meaningful fruition. Around the world, work on children's rights has included moves to ban corporal punishment, end child poverty, consider children and the law, address issues of child labour, and enhance child health (including immunisation, food and the environment).

There is a tendency sometimes to think that such issues apply only to situations in developing countries, but there is work to do on children's rights in the UK too. In a Save the Children study of young children's rights, Alderson (2000) examined children's involvement in decisions which affected them. The study showed how children's contributions were often unrecognised by adults around the UK, and how many adults, due largely to their desire to protect children from danger, denied children basic freedoms to play with their friends.

There are examples of practice where children's rights are a fundamental and guiding principle of curriculum and pedagogy. Such an example can be found in the infant-toddler centres and preschools in Reggio Emilia in Northern Italy. Central concerns are:

> *The rights of children*: the fact that the rights of children are recognised as the rights of all children is the sign of a more accomplished humanity;
>
> *The rights of teachers*: for the teachers, each and every one of them, it is a condition that enhances communication and the comparison of ideas and experiences, all of which enrich the tools of professional evaluation;
>
> *The rights of parents*: participation and research are, in fact, two terms that summarise much of the overall conception of our educational theory. These two terms might also be seen as the best prerequisites for initiating and maintaining a cooperative understanding between parents and teachers, with all the value that is added to the educational prospects of the children. (Malaguzzi, 1996, p. 2)

A second example is found in the argument of daily practice. That is to say that although governments which have signed the UN Convention on the Rights of the Child, thus declaring their commitment to working within their countries to realise and protect children's rights as enshrined in the Convention, much of the reality of putting children's rights into practice lays in the hands of individual practitioners working in services and settings for children and their families.

Securing, upholding and protecting children's rights are the obligation of governments, and of every adult citizen, especially those who work with and for young children. Children's rights means adults responsible for children's services, for housing, health and social services, must ask deep and searching questions. Similarly, practitioners, health workers, teachers, social workers and parents can ask:

- Is every child in this setting seen as equal? Do we treat all children equally and according to their needs whatever their race, colour, religion, sex or nationality?
- Does every child have what he or she needs in order to promote their healthy mental, emotional and physical development?
- Is every child respected here? Do I say and spell their name correctly, do I make efforts to know and understand their background and nationality?
- Do all children have sufficient nutritious food?
- Are all children living in a home which is safe and secure and promotes their well-being?
- Do all children have the medical treatment and care they need?

- Are children's diverse learning and development needs provided for?
- Are all children loved, understood and cared for in ways which meet their needs?
- Do all children have access to the play, learning, and recreation time and space they need?
- Are all children given protection from cruelty, neglect and exploitation?
- Do all children know what it feels like to grow up in a calm and peaceful community?

Curriculum

What young children in England *should* learn has been the subject of continued policy debate, argument and change for decades. Throughout the 1980s and 1990s, government documents endorsed the idea of a specialist curriculum for children under age 5. The Education Reform Act 1988 instigated a curriculum for children aged 5–16 designed and defined in terms of subjects and assessed in terms of attainment targets for each key stage. This curriculum has been the subject of continued controversy, debate and revision since its inception, and changes continue. During the implementation stages of the National Curriculum, the Rumbold Committee (DES, 1989a), reporting on the quality of the educational experience of 3 and 4 year olds in all settings, considered a curriculum 'framework', based on broad areas of experience and learning opportunities which together made up a balanced and broad curriculum, was the best way to proceed for young children under 5 years of age. Her Majesty's Inspectorate (HMI) (DES, 1989b) had already set forward this view so far as nursery schools and classes were concerned, and there was some broad consensus about its appropriateness.

The present curriculum for children aged from birth to 5, the *Early Years Foundation Stage* (DfE, 2012), had its beginnings in funding arrangements initiated by the government in 1996. The document *Desirable Outcomes of Nursery Education* (DfEE, 1996) was not so much a curriculum as a set of criteria for assessment of children or inspection of provision. Government-funded provision for 3–5 year-olds was to be required to demonstrate how it enabled children to meet the stated outcomes in what were termed: *personal and social development; language and literacy; mathematics; knowledge and understanding of the world; physical development;* and *creative development.*

The *Desirable Outcomes* document contained a passing reference to play as a medium for learning and placed clear emphasis on socialising children for school and achievement in literacy and numeracy. The intended progression from pre-compulsory to compulsory education at level 2 of

Key Stage 1 was clearly set out (DfEE, 1996, p. 10), as was the purpose of such provision: 'to provide a foundation for later achievement' (p. 1).

Hot on the heels of this narrow definition of children's early achievements came plans for the assessment of children on entry to school. *The National Framework for Baseline Assessment* (SCAA, 1997) was introduced in September 1998, requiring all schools to carry out a Baseline Assessment of children within the first half-term of their beginning compulsory schooling (regardless of whether or not the children were themselves of compulsory school age). Strong protests and professional dissatisfaction eventually led to the withdrawal of Baseline Assessment in favour of a more holistic and formative assessment process for 3–5 year-olds in the form of the Foundation Stage Profile (QCA, 2008b). These were later revised as the Early Years Foundation Stage and the Early Years Foundation Stage Profile (DCSF, 2008) and again to the present curriculum and its assessment (DfE, 2012). Within two decades, early education in the UK moved from no officially defined, recognised or required *curriculum* to an imposed assessment of achievements (often before 5 years of age) at the start of school.

Whatever the officially prescribed curriculum, and in whatever geographical location, effective educators around the world must focus not just on areas of learning, but also on ways of extending and linking different strands of knowledge and understanding and experience – on continuity and progression within and across different areas of learning. Such teaching can give young children opportunities for learning and development that are rich and full and create an experience of early education that is satisfying in holistic terms and reaches beyond official descriptors of required learning and extends the parameters of knowledge.

A balanced, broad, relevant and differentiated curriculum is much more than rhetoric. It is a sound philosophy of curriculum entitlement for all children who can be taught and can learn according to their needs and in tune with their potential, and is rooted in the work of many teachers and educationalists. Freire reminds us of the need for children to re-invent, rather than simply to be told: 'Knowledge emerges only through invention and re-invention, through the restless, impatient, continuing, hopeful inquiry human beings pursue in the world, with the world, and with each other' (Freire, 1970, p. 53). Put another way, we could say that children have to re-invent the wheel!

John Dewey took the position that process was as much (if not more) part of the learning as the outcome:

> The individual who has a question, which being really a question to him, instigates his curiosity, which feeds his eagerness for information. Whatever initiative and imaginative vision he possesses will be called into play. (Dewey, 1916, pp. 304–5)

What Freire and Dewey, among others, emphasised was the action of the individual in their own learning and the importance of processes of thinking and doing. Subjects are one way of categorising elements of knowledge into convenient groupings so that teaching and assessment can be managed and curriculum discussed, but this is not the only way of learning about things and the sometimes constrained compartmentalisation of learning into subjects can be less than helpful in terms of understanding and challenging young children's thinking. The irrelevance of subject-based approaches to teaching young children is ably demonstrated by Hurst and Joseph, who wrote:

> ... for young children a 'subject-based' approach to a curriculum is inappropriate, as it goes against the ways in which children think and learn. The programmes of study in the present National Curriculum are divided into areas – Art; Geography; English; Mathematics; Physical Education; Science; Information Technology and Design Technology – and this goes against the grain of what we have been saying. On the other hand, the holistic way of learning *is* partly recognised within the National Curriculum. The notion of 'cross-curricular themes, dimensions and skills' subscribes to the fact that bringing different kinds of subject knowledge together can be the most fruitful way of promoting learning, and those practitioners who are involved with carrying out the National Curriculum would do their children a great favour if they made the most of that acknowledgement. (Hurst and Joseph, 1998, pp. 22–3)

In reality, young children do not think in subjects, or 'areas' of learning for that matter. Neither do adults. Human beings think in terms of situations, puzzles, problems to be solved, questions to be answered; it is the same for adults and children alike. And, as Socrates said: 'Wisdom begins with wonder.' Young children are thinking, talking and applying their existing knowledge; the children attend to the task in hand. Children do not analyse their knowledge in terms of subjects, but rather they explore – with wonder – the questions that they generate in their everyday environments.

As we have said, it has been argued that early education, at its best, is inclusive education (Nutbrown, 1998), though the important phrase here is 'at its best'. The best of early education includes: developmentally appropriate practice, observation-based pedagogy and assessment; close parental involvement; equality of access to a differentiated curriculum and a multi-professional, cross-agency approach to provision. If we take England as an example, this may well have been an expected state of affairs during the 1970s and 1980s. However, inclusive education in England came under threat during the 1990s when schools and other settings faced: inadequate funding; increasingly centralised control of curriculum; negative attitudes across society towards disability; a lack of action on human rights in general and, more specifically, on children's rights, and a lack of appropriate and funded professional development for teachers and other early years professionals (Nutbrown, 1998).

These factors and the increasing control over curriculum in the early years could have threatened inclusive curricular practices and, in the process, created difficulty with learning for some children. For as soon as *Desirable Outcomes of Nursery Education* (SCAA, 1996) was published, there were inevitably children who did not reach those targets. Similarly, as soon as individual targets for achievement at 4 years old were prescribed (SCAA, 1997), children were identified who did not reach those given targets. Such children were 'below the norm' – a case of 'targets' actually creating learning difficulties. However, the subsequent curriculum guidance in England, the *Curriculum Guidance for the Foundation Stage* (QCA/DfES, 2008a), took an inclusive stance, defining inclusion in a broad sense and stating that the guidance was:

> ... intended to help practitioners plan to meet the diverse needs of all children so that most will achieve and some, where appropriate, will go beyond the early learning goals by the end of the foundation stage. (p. 5)

The guidance was based on several principles, including that:

> ... no child should be excluded or disadvantaged because of ethnicity, culture or religion, home language, family background, special educational needs, disability, gender or ability. (p. 11)

With regard to 'children with special educational needs and disabilities' (p. 18), the curriculum guidance for England encourages multi-agency and multi-professional working and the close involvement of parents so that learning needs are identified early and inclusive practices developed:

> Practitioners will need to plan for each child's individual learning requirements, including those children who need additional support or have particular needs or disabilities. The focus should be on removing barriers for children where these already exist and on preventing learning difficulties from developing. Early years practitioners have a key role to play in working with parents to identify learning needs and respond quickly to any area of particular difficulty, and to develop an effective strategy to meet these needs, making good use of individual educational plans, so that later difficulties can be avoided. (p. 18)

In 2007, changes in curriculum guidance and statutory requirements for provision for children under age 5 led to an incorporation of curriculum content which might be described as addressing issues of citizenship. For example, the Early Years Foundation Stage (DCSF, 2007), which became statutory in September 2008, states (under what is called *Positive Relationships: Respecting Each Other*) that:

> When each person is valued for who they are and differences are appreciated, everyone feels included and understood, whatever their personality, abilities, ethnic background or culture. (para 2.1)

And in the section identified as *Enabling Environments: The Learning Environment* it is suggested that:

> When children feel confident in the environment they are willing to try things out, knowing that effort is valued. (para 3.3)

These two statements can be read as a clear assertion that inclusion, citizenship and belonging are key to current early years policy in England. But what does *'valuing each child for who they are'* look like? And what factors help children to *'feel confident in the environment'*?

In 2011 the Tickell Review of the Early Years Foundation Stage (Tickell, 2011) recommended revisions to the early years curriculum:

> Alongside the three prime areas of:
>
> - personal, social and emotional development,
> - communication and language and
> - physical development
>
> I propose four specific areas in which the prime skills are applied:
>
> - literacy,
> - mathematics,
> - expressive arts and design, and
> - understanding the world. (para 3.28)

The Review also recast the place of play in the early years curriculum:

> I therefore recommend that playing and exploring, active learning, and creating and thinking critically, are highlighted in the EYFS as three characteristics of effective teaching and learning ... (para 3.29)

The revised EYFS was published in 2012 (DfE, 2012) and, while it included many mentions of the term 'learning', there was little said about 'play'.

Attention to targets and individual achievement through a government-prescribed and adult-dominated curriculum is not, however, the experience of all countries. Experiences from Denmark, with its minimally prescribed curriculum, New Zealand's *Te Whariki* (NZ Ministry of Education, 1995) and

Steiner-Waldorf education, with its emphasis on holistic education, for example, demonstrate that alternatives are possible and can be effective.

What could help to further inclusivity in the early years is a rubric of developmentally appropriate, respectful curricula and pedagogical practices where children learn together in diverse and challenging social situations, experience difference and learn negotiation and respect. At the core of these values of curriculum and pedagogy is play.

Play

Play in early childhood education and care is a central component of children's experiences and, for them, is a fundamental way of learning. Lowenfeld states:

> Play in childhood is an exceedingly complex phenomenon. It is an activity which combines into a single whole, very different strands of thought and experience. Many of these persist in adult life. (1935)

The word 'play' is used liberally and with the assumption that its meaning is understood, though it can be seen to mean different things to different people, and the use of play in national policy documents in the UK may not match its use by, for example, Steiner-Waldorf teachers. Many famous pioneers of early childhood education – Montessori, Steiner, Froebel, Isaacs, the MacMillan sisters – saw play as central to their work in developing nursery and kindergarten curricula. Play has, in turn, been heralded as the essential means through which children learn, and yet play is also castigated and sidelined in favour of a more teacher-directed way of learning so that young children should 'work' in school. A perceived reduction in opportunities for children to play (in early years and school settings *and* at home) has also led to concerns over children's well-being, health and fitness, with physical and creative activity being replaced by the overuse of technological toys and games (Alliance for Childhood, 2004; Early Childhood Action, 2012).

In their seminal work, Manning and Sharp (1977) explain the purpose of their 'Play' project:

> The idea of the project first arose because of the difficulties which many teachers were experiencing in using play in the classroom. Although accepting that children learn and develop through play and that play is a motivating force for children's learning, many teachers are pressurised by the very full first school curriculum and large classes to neglect play as a means of teaching. They leave children to play on their own. In addition,

> many parents' expectations are that children will 'work' when they come
> to school, not 'play'. (p. 7)

Some 35 years later, many early years teachers continue to struggle to 'fit'
play into their pedagogic repertoire and, though play is now reinstated in
terms of the early years, some practitioners still lack the necessary skills
and confidence to support children's play. In 1997 the British Educational
Research Association (BERA) reviewed research on early years pedagogy,
curriculum and adult roles and, perhaps significantly, found few examples
of recent studies. Of play, the review stated:

> Several key studies have provided an evidence base on the quality of play,
> its educational benefits, and the pedagogy of play, in the contexts of pre-
> school and school settings ... Most of these studies did not focus specifi-
> cally on play, but on broader curriculum and pedagogical processes, of
> which play was an integral part. Their findings were critical of the quality
> of play, the dislocation between rhetoric and reality of play, the extent to
> which play and learning were linked, the role of the adults in children's
> play, and how play was utilised towards educational outcomes. The con-
> sistent picture to emerge from these studies is that play in practice has
> been limited in frequency, duration and quality, with teachers and other
> adults too often adopting a reactive 'watching and waiting' approach.
> (BERA, Early Years Special Interest Group 1997, p. 14)

The propensity of children the world over to play and the perceived
benefits of play to children's holistic development provides a strong case
for the professional exploration of the role of play in supporting
children's well-being, development and learning.

In recent years more attention has been paid to children from birth
to 3 and their play, too, is an issue for many practitioners. Manning-
Morton and Thorp (2004) examine the importance of play for children
under 3 years of age and identify the crucial role of adults in such play
in supporting and developing play experiences. Play is seen in relation
to all aspects of a child's day, as integral to and as part of an holistic
approach to early education and care for very young children. Questions about the efficacy of play as a pedagogical tool remain and suc-
cessive governments have shown varied degrees of commitment to
early years and school curriculum in relation to play. In the light of
this, Christmas (2005) was moved to ask the teachers and other staff
in her small village school for their views on play, and found that
while people generally thought it was 'OK to play', worries over the
play/work balance for young children still remained.

Of play, the Tickell Review (2011, para 3.9) said: 'I therefore recommend that playing and exploring, active learning, and creating and
thinking critically, are highlighted in the EYFS as three characteristics of

effective teaching and learning...'. The Review went on to recommend a policy perspective on play which is multifaceted and does not see play as something wholly in and of itself, but as a natural process of childhood which can be harnessed and purposively used to extend learning.

Developmentally appropriate practice

Bredekamp and Copple's (1997) advocacy of a *developmentally appropriate approach* to an early years curriculum is defined as:

> curriculum and pedagogy based upon agreed stages of children's development. It is a framework of principles and guidelines for best practice in the care and education of young children, birth through age 8.[1]

and

> [In] **DAP** [Developmentally Appropriate Practice] ... teachers integrate the many dimensions of their knowledge base. They must know about child development and the implication of this knowledge for how to teach, the content of the curriculum – what to teach and when – how to assess what children have learned, and how to adapt curriculum and instruction to children's individual strengths, needs and interests. (NAEYC, 1996)

The term 'developmentally appropriate practice', in the USA, is taken to refer to early childhood programmes serving children from birth to 8 years. NAEYC documentation states that:

> In their decision making, effective early childhood educators keep in mind the desired outcomes for children's learning and development, and they understand that:
>
> Knowledge must inform decision making
>
> Goals must be challenging and achievable
>
> Teaching must be intentional to be effective.[2]

> Twelve key principles of child development and learning inform developmentally appropriate practice in early childhood programmes serving children from birth to 8 years. These principles cover: the interrelation of the physical, social, emotional, and cognitive domains of development; sequential patterns and varying rates of development; the influence of multiple social and cultural contexts; children's active role in learning; the importance of interaction; play as a vehicle for development; the

---

[1]Developmentally Appropriate Practice, www.naeyc.org/DAP

[2]See www.naeyc.org/dap/core

place of practice and mastery; children's ways of showing what they know, and the importance of a safe and supporting community for learning. (NAEYC, 1996)

Such practice, taken to its ultimate form – where practice is routinely adapted to 'children's individual strengths, needs and interests' – negates the needs for discussion of 'additional needs' and even the idea of special educational needs.

Katz (1995) suggests that in developmentally appropriate approaches to curriculum, decisions 'about what should be learned and how it would best be learned depend on what we know of the learner's developmental status and our understanding of the relationships between early experience and subsequent development' (p. 109). Of course, views of *development* and what constitutes *appropriate* development are always contestable. However, taken together with Vygotsky's (1978) notion of the *Zone of Proximal Development*, it is possible to identify ways in which supporting children's learning can be informed and appropriate to their stage of learning.

Such questions have underpinned many studies which have sought to inform curriculum and programme development. These include Athey's (2007) work on schematic development, Nutbrown's (2010) study of curriculum development based on schematic theory, Reggio Emilia preschools' development of communities of learning through multiple modes of expression (Malaguzzi, 1996; Abbott and Nutbrown, 2001; Edwards et al., 2001), and the curriculum *Te Whariki*, developed in New Zealand, which promotes equality of opportunity in contexts of diversity (New Zealand Ministry of Education, 1995). The Early Years Learning Framework in Australia, 'Being, Belonging and Becoming' (AGDEEW, 2009), stated that:

> Early childhood educators who are committed to equity believe in all children's capacities to succeed, regardless of diverse circumstances and abilities. Children progress well when they, their parents and educators hold high expectations for their achievement in learning. Educators recognise and respond to barriers to children achieving educational success. In response, they challenge practices that contribute to inequities and make curriculum decisions that promote inclusion and participation of all children. By developing their professional knowledge and skills, and working in partnership with children, families, communities, other services and agencies, they continually strive to find equitable and effective ways to ensure that all children have opportunities to achieve learning outcomes. (pp. 12–13)

Furthermore, the Australian Framework defined inclusion thus:

> **Inclusion:** involves taking into account all children's social, cultural and linguistic diversity (including learning styles, abilities, disabilities, gender, family circumstances and geographic location) in curriculum decision-making processes. The intent is to ensure that all children's experiences

are recognised and valued. The intent is also to ensure that all children have equitable access to resources and participation, and opportunities to demonstrate their learning and to value difference. (p. 45)

Such studies and policy developments are evidence of the continuing global quest for ways of creating curriculum which satisfactorily meets the developmental needs of all young children. If anything, such approaches are even more necessary in the design of education and care of young children with learning difficulties.

Assessment

Assessment of children's progress and learning is, of course, part of any educator's role. The term is used in multiple contexts and carries many meanings of both purpose and practice. However, there remains the assumption that everyone understands what assessment means and yet confusion over terminology continues throughout various policy developments in early years assessment.

Nutbrown (2011) has suggested three different purposes for assessment in the early years, arguing that different tools are needed for different purposes: assessment for teaching and learning; assessment for management and accountability; and assessment for research. *Assessment for teaching and learning* is that which is most obviously useful in supporting young children's learning and development, the process of identifying the details of children's knowledge, skills and understanding in order to build a detailed picture of the child's development and subsequent learning needs. Nutbrown argues that several aspects need to be addressed by practitioners if assessment is to work for children (Box 2.5).

Assessment of young children raises a number of concerns in relation to their well-being and self-esteem. Roberts (2006, p.113) writes:

> Assessment and recording arrangements carry a world of hidden messages for children and parents. Is a positive model used, one which identifies children's special strengths as well as areas for support? Is there accurate and detailed information about children? Do adults make sure that children share their successes, both with their parents and with each other?
>
> These questions raise some of the issues which have a direct bearing on how children learn to see themselves. Attention to these sorts of details may have a profound effect on children's approach to learning. Our attention to them is surely the entitlement of every child.

Box 2.5   Issues in assessment

- *Clarity of purpose* – why are children being assessed?

- *Fitness for purpose* – is the assessment instrument or process appropriate?

- *Authenticity* – do the assessment tasks reflect processes of children's learning and their interests?

- *Informed practitioners* – are practitioners appropriately trained and supported?

- *Child involvement* – how can children be fittingly involved in assessment of their learning?

- *Respectful assessment* – are assessments fair and honest, with appropriate concern for children's well-being and involvement?

- *Parental involvement* – do parents contribute to their child's assessment?

(Adapted from Nutbrown, 2011, p. 14)

Conclusion

The issues which we have identified in this chapter will be revisited throughout the book as we consider aspects of inclusion from various viewpoints and policy perspectives.

Workshop 2 Mapping your territories of inclusion and exclusion

In Box 2.1 (on page 9) we listed 18 arenas for inclusion/exclusion. Thinking of a particular early years setting or families using early years education and care services, in what ways do any of these apply to the families and children you know? How, for example, has the age of a child or a parent led to exclusion? Have you been aware of the home language of a family restricting their inclusion in the culture of your early years setting? Does parental employment make a difference to their inclusion in the life and culture of the provision?

Reflecting on questions such as these (which might be prompted by the list in Box 2.1), discuss your thoughts with colleagues and consider how exclusive tendencies might be reduced or eliminated in order to create a more inclusive culture in your setting.

Keep your notes from this workshop – they may be useful as you work through other workshops at the end of each chapter.

Policy points

In this section we identify key elements of policy across the four devolved administrations of the UK as they relate to the issues discussed throughout this chapter.

Play

'Play is a central component of children's experiences and a key means by which they learn' (Nutbrown, 2011, p. 114). Policy documents for England, Northern Ireland, Scotland and Wales reflect this understanding in making particular reference to the importance of play for young children. The policies of the four countries of the United Kingdom concur:

In England
'Each area of learning and development must be implemented through planned, purposeful play and through a mix of adult-led and child-initiated activity. Play is essential for children's development, building their confidence as they learn to explore, to think about problems, and relate to others.' (DfE, 2012, p. 6)

In Scotland
'Play is very powerful in promoting children's development and learning ... children need the freedom to play, to practise skills, explore the world around them, and develop knowledge and understanding in their own way and in their own time.' (Learning and Teaching Scotland, 2010, p. 72)

'Planning should demonstrate the principles for curriculum design: challenge and enjoyment; breadth; progression; depth; personalisation and choice; coherence; relevance.' (Scottish Government, 2008, p. 8)

In Northern Ireland
'Children are involved in play that is challenging, takes account of their developmental stage and needs and builds on their own interests and experiences.' (CCEA, 2006, p. 6)

In Wales
'Children learn through first-hand experiential activities with the serious business of "play" providing the vehicle.' (Welsh Assembly Government, 2008, p. 4)

'For children, play can be (and often is) a very serious business.' (Welsh Assembly Government, 2008, p. 6)

Further reading

Booth, T., Ainscow, M. and Kingston, D. (2006) *Index for Inclusion: Developing Play, Learning and Participation in Early Years and Childcare* (2nd edition). Bristol: Centre for Studies in Inclusive Education. The Index is available from: CSIE 1, Redland Close, Elm Lane, Redland, Bristol BS6 6UE.

Swadener, B.B., Grant, C.A., Mitakidou, S. and Tressou, E. (2009) *Beyond Pedagogies of Exclusion in Diverse Childhood Contexts: Transnational Challenges* (Critical Cultural Studies of Childhood). New York: Palgrave Macmillan.

3

Key studies on Special Educational Needs

Introduction

Having established the broad terrain of inclusion in the early years, we must acknowledge that while the specific issues which relate to children with learning difficulties or to those defined as having 'special educational needs' are only part of the full picture of inclusion in the early years, they are often distinct and, without doubt, important. Our ongoing search of the literature on inclusion in early years reveals that though the field is growing, there is relatively little work on *inclusion* which is not *SEN and/ or disability* focused.

Reflecting this almost exclusive occupation with learning difficulties, therefore, in this chapter we review international research relating to issues which connect three important themes: Early Childhood Education and Care, Special Educational Needs and Inclusion of children with learning difficulties (see Figure 3.1).

Within the three intersecting fields in Figure 3.1, several issues, some of which have already been raised in Chapter 2, emerge:

- Definitions of SEN
- Inclusive education and children with learning difficulties
- Inclusion and emotional and behavioural difficulties
- Inclusive policies and exclusive practices

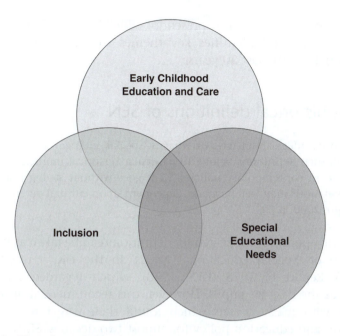

Figure 3.1   Three intersecting themes

Viewpoints from research

About ten years ago, in a review of the literature on teachers' attitudes towards integration/inclusion, Avramidis and Norwich (2002) showed that attitudes were generally positive but that the nature and severity of children's needs strongly influenced teachers' dispositions towards inclusive practices. This is in keeping with Clough's (1999) earlier indications of the 'hierarchies of tolerance' which generally characterise teacher perspectives. Avramidis and Norwich (2002, p. 134) drew on three major factors: child-related variables; teacher-related variables; context/environment. These factors underpin our review of the international literature in relation to attitudes and responses towards children with Special Educational Needs and Inclusive Education in the early years.

The focus in this book is on early education but, for children with learning difficulties, this phase is just the beginning of a long road within educational provision. For this reason, we have included in this selective overview of research, relevant findings from studies involving older pupils and we also reach into the recent historical past in order to try to understand current policy developments. This chapter draws on selected recent research into preschool education and SEN in international contexts and identifies key themes that have permeated the research field in the last 20 years.

Recent historical definitions of SEN

> Consensual ideas about who or what is 'special' change, sometimes rapidly; all such definitions belong to particular historical moments and are reflected in contemporary policies. ... It goes without saying that other interpretations may well be made, dependent upon cultural determinants. (Clough, 2000, p. 5)

One starting point for the search for definitions can be taken as the policy inception of 'Special Educational Needs' in the UK, a result of the Warnock Report of 1978 (DES, 1978), which regarded mainstream settings as the best for pupils. However, this recommendation was shot through with many *caveats* which found their way into subsequent legislation and education policy for almost two decades. Since the 1978 Warnock Report, there have been many changes in policy and practice in the UK: the Education Reform Act 1988 (DfE, 1988), which heralded the National Curriculum; national assessment throughout primary schools; a specific Code of Practice for the Identification and Assessment of SEN (DfE, 1994); the introduction of Baseline Assessment of 4 year olds (SCAA, 1997); the Foundation Stage curriculum (for 3–5+ year olds) (QCA/DfEE, 2000, 2008a) and Foundation Stage Profile for assessment of children 3–5+ years (QCA/DfES, 2008b) and, in 2012, the revised Early Years Foundation Stage (DfE, 2012). Throughout this period a series of Codes of Practice for SEN had been issued and new posts of responsibility for SEN were created whereby every school was required to appoint a Special Educational Needs Co-ordinator (SENCO). Educators in preschool and in special education in the UK have, arguably, been at the forefront of educational change for some 20 years (Nutbrown, 2002a), a period which has also seen an increasing emphasis on accountability, curriculum regulation, parental rights and responsibilities, and interagency partnership.

A radical and far-reaching cross-governmental policy change for England was the Children Act 2004. Endorsed jointly by no less than 16 government ministers responsible at some level for coordinating the delivery of services for children, young people and families, the Children Act 2004 provided 'the legislative foundation for whole-system reform to support this long-term and ambitious programme' (DfES, 2004, p. 2). New statutory duties were outlined and accountabilities for children's services, at government and local authority levels, were clarified. The introduction stated:

Every Child Matters: Change for Children sets out the national framework for local change programmes to build services around the needs of children and young people so that we maximise opportunity and minimise risk. The services that reach every child and young person have a crucial role to play in shifting the focus from dealing with the consequences of difficulties in children's lives to preventing things from going wrong in the first place. The transformation that we need can only be delivered through local leaders working together in strong partnership with local communities on a programme of change. (DfES, 2004, p. 2)

It was recognised that such an ambitious policy to improve outcomes for children could only succeed if there was radical change in the system of children's services, including:

- the improvement and integration of universal services – in early years settings, schools and the health service;
- more specialised help to promote opportunity, prevent problems and act early and effectively if and when problems arise;
- the reconfiguration of services around the child and family in one place, for example, children's centres, extended schools and the bringing together of professionals in multi-disciplinary teams;
- dedicated and enterprising leadership at all levels of the system;
- the development of a shared sense of responsibility across agencies for safeguarding children and protecting them from harm; and
- listening to children, young people and their families when assessing and planning service provision, as well as in face-to-face delivery. (DfES, 2004, p. 2)

The Children Act 2004 laid the ground to establish (for children in England):

- a Children's Commissioner to champion the views and interests of children and young people;
- a duty on Local Authorities to make arrangements to promote co-operation between agencies and other appropriate bodies (such as voluntary and community organisations) in order to improve children's well-being (where well-being is defined by reference to the five outcomes), and a duty on key partners to take part in the co-operation arrangements;
- a duty on key agencies to safeguard and promote the welfare of children;
- a duty on Local Authorities to set up Local Safeguarding Children Boards and on key partners to take part;
- provision for indexes or databases containing basic information about children and young people to enable better sharing of information;

- a requirement for a single Children and Young People's Plan to be drawn up by each Local Authority;
- a requirement on Local Authorities to appoint a Director of Children's Services and designate a Lead Member;
- the creation of an integrated inspection framework and the conduct of Joint Area Reviews to assess local areas' progress in improving outcomes; and
- provisions relating to foster care, private fostering and the education of children in care. (DfES, 2004, p. 8)

Every Child Matters: Change for Children (DfES, 2004) identified five outcomes: be healthy; stay safe; enjoy and achieve; make a positive contribution; achieve economic well-being. Each of these outcomes had five aims attached for children and young people, though several policy moves later, these outcomes still hold meaningful messages for practice. Table 3.1 identifies the first three outcomes which apply more obviously to the youngest children (though some of the aims relate more to older children and young people).

As can be seen in Table 3.1, the responsibilities of 'parents, carers and families' were made explicit in helping to achieve these outcomes.

Table 3.1   Outcomes for children in *Every Child Matters*

Be Healthy	Physically healthy
	Mentally and emotionally healthy
	Sexually healthy
	Healthy lifestyles
	Choose not to take illegal drugs
	Parents, carers and families promote healthy choices
Stay safe	Safe from maltreatment, neglect, violence and sexual exploitation
	Safe from accidental injury and death
	Safe from bullying and discrimination
	Safe from crime and anti-social behaviour in and out of school
	Have security, stability and are cared for
	Parents, carers and families provide safe homes and stability
Enjoy and share	Ready for school
	Attend and enjoy school
	Achieve stretching national educational standards at primary school
	Achieve personal and social development and enjoy recreation
	Achieve stretching national educational standards at secondary school
	Parents, carers and families support learning

Source: DfES, 2004, p. 9

The model put forward by government in order to realise these out-comes for all children was encapsulated in what was called the 'Children's Trust'. With the 'Outcomes for children and young people' and parents, families and community at the centre, key processes in the model are: integrated 'front line' delivery; integrated processes; integrated strategy; and 'inter-agency governance'. Integration of agencies and cross-governance was central to the strategy at the core of the Children Act 2004. The Act aimed to provide 'personalised and high quality, integrated universal services' (DfES, 2004, p. 14). Specifically, in terms of the early years, this meant:

> Early years and childcare provision gives a good start to young children's development as well as appropriate support to their parents. The Government has made significant progress in giving a good start to families with very young children through Sure Start local programmes and children's centres, combining health and family support with early education and childcare. ... Community participation has been a key to the success of current provision and will be critical to the success of future arrangements. (DfES, 2004, p. 14, para 3.6)

The Act promoted a greater emphasis on integrated services which collaborate to provide targeted and specialist services for children with additional needs, 'such as those with disabilities, those whose parents have mental health problems or those who need to be protected from harm' (DfES, 2004, p. 15).

Three key factors were identified as specific needs for such children:

- high-quality multi-agency assessment;
- a wide range of specialist services available close to home; and
- effective case management by a lead professional working as part of a multi-disciplinary team. (DfES, 2004, p. 15)

A Common Assessment Framework (CAF) (to be implemented by 2008) was planned to provide a user-friendly assessment of all the child's individual, family and community needs. Such assessments were designed to be built up over time and, with consent, shared between practitioners. The aim of the CAF was to 'promote more effective, earlier identification of children's additional needs and improve multi-agency working' by:

- improving the quality of referrals between agencies by making them more evidence-based;
- helping embed a common language about the needs of children and young people;
- promoting the appropriate sharing of information; and
- reducing the number and duration of different assessment processes which children and young people need to undergo. (DfES, 2004, p. 15)

Box 3.1 (from *Every Child Matters*) illustrates how such collaborative assessment can improve things for children and their families.

Box 3.1 Shropshire ISA trailblazer – early intervention

Before co-ordinated early intervention

M had been receiving help at nursery school from the Behaviour Support Service due to his aggressive behaviour. However, over the summer his behaviour worsened and his mother was concerned that the transition to reception class meant he would not get the same level of support. She contacted the Information Sharing and Assessment co-ordinator, who agreed to liaise with other agencies. A check on the data held for M revealed incomplete records, particularly of mental health issues; M's Health Visitor confirmed concerns about his sleep routines and an outstanding referral for speech therapy, while the school revealed concerns about M and his mother's difficulties.

After co-ordinated early intervention

The school undertook a Common Assessment with M's mother and from that planned how services could come together to form 'a team around the child', including an education Welfare Assistant, a Health Visitor and a teacher. As a result, the Education Welfare Assistant worked with M at home and at school, a re-referral for speech therapy was made, and the Health Visitor continued to offer support to his mother, suggesting strategies for dealing with his behaviour. M's class teacher acted as the first point of contact for the family and information was shared on request with the other specialists about M's vulnerabilities and his behavioural difficulties. Due to this integrated approach to identifying and addressing the causes of M's behaviour, M's family now feels they are receiving co-ordinated support that meets his needs. His re-referral for speech therapy was prioritised due to his needs being set within a broader context of his educational and social development, and the team continues to work with M and his family to achieve more improvement.

(DfES, 2004, p. 16)

While the Children Act 2004 applied to *all* children in England, it was clear that its impact would be most obvious where children were vulnerable, in particular those who were believed to be at risk and children with learning difficulties and additional needs.

So far we have discussed policy on the inclusion of children with learning difficulties from various UK policy perspectives. From these UK positions and in the context of increasing Europeanisation and the potential transferability of the workforce, it seemed obvious that questions of what is happening in the rest of Europe should be asked. Of course, parallel activities have been taking place in many countries in Europe as educators and policy makers seek answers to the difficult questions surrounding the education of vulnerable pupils – vulnerable because they are young, and vulnerable also because these are perceptions variably of their 'difference' from many of their peers and of the adults in the school community. Throughout all of this policy development there remains one policy/practice constant – the perpetual reality of learning difficulties. Such a reality was expressed in the UK Green Paper of 1997:

> There are strong educational, as well as social and moral grounds for educating children with special educational needs with their peers. We aim to increase the level and quality of inclusion within mainstream schools, while protecting and enhancing specialist provision for those who need it. (DfEE, 1997, p. 27)

The 2009 *Guide for Parents of Children with Special Educational Needs* (DCSF, 2009) drew attention to the importance of the Code of Practice in identifying, assessing and providing for children who had additional needs, in order to support their learning. It stresses the importance of the 1996 Education Act, in terms of entitlement of children with difficulties. Following the formation of the Coalition government after the election in 2010, there appeared to be a policy vacuum, and some details of existing policy – whilst not yet changed, were identified as not necessarily being current policy. For some time, some current government policy web pages still carried the statement:

All statutory guidance and legislation published on this site continues to reflect the current legal position unless indicated otherwise.

Pages without the following disclaimer have been created or updated since the formation of the new Government on 11 May 2010, and reflect current policy.

> This page may not reflect Government policy. More information.

Pages with this disclaimer were created before 11 May but have been retained for a number of reasons. For example they may:

- continue to reflect the current legal position; or
- provide useful historic or reference information; or
- provide a time series of research or analysis over a number of years; or
- be reference materials or case studies that schools' or children's workforces have told us they find useful.

This disclaimer will be kept in place until content is amended or removed by the Department.

You can get further information by contacting the Department.

Figure 3.2 Example of policy disclaimer

Source: www.education.gov.uk/help/AboutContent

This statement made it difficult to summarise and critique government policy with any degree of reliability.

When early education settings, schools, local authorities and health and social services decide how they will help children with special educational needs, they should always consider what the SEN Code says.

The most important law dealing with special education is the 1996 Education Act. A Special Educational Needs Code of Practice gives practical guidance on how to identify and assess children with Special educational needs. All early education settings, state schools and local authorities must take account of this Code when they are dealing with children who have special educational needs. Health and social services must also take account of the Code when helping local authorities. This means that, when early education settings, schools, local authorities and health and social services decide how they will help children with special educational needs, they should always consider what the Code Says.

Figure 3.3 Example of lack of clarity on policy

Policy developments in Europe

Inclusive education and children with learning difficulties

Nearly 20 years ago, the *Salamanca Statement: Framework for Action for Special Needs Education* (UNESCO, 1994) was drawn up by representatives from 92 governments and 25 international organisations. The statement called for inclusion to be the norm and the conference adopted a 'Framework for Action' which would require all children to be accommodated in ordinary schools, regardless of their physical, intellectual, social, emotional, linguistic or other conditions. According to the Framework, national and local policies should stipulate that disabled children attend the neighbourhood school 'that would be attended if the child did not have a disability' (p. 17). The statement insists on the provision of education for all 'within the regular system'.

> Regular schools with this inclusive orientation are the most effective means of combating discriminatory attitudes, creating welcoming communities, building on an inclusive society and achieving education for all; moreover, they provide an effective education to the majority of children and improve the efficiency and ultimately the cost-effectiveness of the entire education system. (Centre for Studies in Inclusive Education, 1995, p. 8)

The *Salamanca Statement* had economic as well as sociological, political and educational goals. It was bold and important, but as Clough argued:

> In this multinational urge *for* inclusion lies the danger of physical *inclusion* but curricular and emotional *exclusion* unless children are included for and of themselves, by teachers who are professionally and personally equipped to provide appropriate education for all. For inclusion is about a radical deal more than physical location. (1998, p. 5)

Vakil, Freeman and Swim (2003) take up this theme, calling for inclusive education which features developmentally appropriate practice (Bredekamp and Copple, 1997) and culturally appropriate practices as well as specifically tailored support. Reflecting on special educational needs in the Reggio Emilia preschools of Northern Italy (a country where national legislation has promoted 'integrated' schooling since 1977), Phillips (2001) notes the lack of overt reference – an apparent *de-emphasis* – on perfecting the physical environment for 'access' but an emphasis on inclusive practice, whereby children who are disabled have priority in being allocated places in preschool provision. This reflects the pedagogy of 'community' rather than the 'individual' and perhaps it is this that leads Nurse (2001) to observe:

> My impression of Reggio Emilia's response to children with special needs is that the preschools minimise the effects of disability and a slower rate of learning because the learning environment matches the developmental and social needs of the individual child. ... A difference between the system in the UK and the Reggio response is the commitment to children learning as a group, from each other. ... Reggio Emilia is a stable, prosperous and cohesive community. The preschools are a highly regarded part of that community which in turn values the group experience they offer to young children.

> Provision is local so the children are not placed in distant centres which isolate them and their families from their own community. (p. 68)

Rates of inclusion (however defined) across Europe vary greatly. In a study of practice of inclusion in 14 European countries, Meijer (1998) demonstrated that the numbers of pupils in special schools and classes varied between less than 1% and over 4% with special education systems in north-western Europe being more prevalent than those in Scandinavia and southern Europe. Meijer also shows how, during the 1990s, most European countries changed their laws with regard to the education of pupils with learning difficulties. According to Meijer, the success of integration or inclusion depends to a great extent on existing education structures and it appears to be of greater concern when investment in special school provision is high.

A thematic review of Early Childhood Education and Care (ECEC) in 12 countries carried out by the Organisation for Economic Cooperation and Development (OECD) identified, as a key element of successful ECEC policy, 'a universal approach to access, with particular attention to children in need of special support' (OECD, 2001, p. 130). Such a policy, suggests the OECD, features 'an inclusive and flexible approach to diversity, without compromising quality' (p. 130). The OECD review suggested that such an approach means:

> ... mainstreaming children with special educational needs, whenever this is deemed in the best interests of the child. When inclusion is not feasible, more targeted programmes and projects can be developed to provide equality of educational opportunity and promote social integration for children living in disadvantaged communities. (OECD, 2001, p. 130)

Inclusion and emotional and behavioural difficulties

Even in the early years, the 'type' of difficulty greatly influences the willingness and capacity of early childhood educators to include children in ordinary mainstream settings. Pupil behaviour and the education of pupils with emotional and behavioural difficulties (EBD) is, of course, a uniform international issue. Behaviours which go against the social conventions of schools and communities threaten the social order (even in the early years the calm of a kindergarten can be shattered when the behaviour of children with EBD confronts the usual system of quiet discipline and order). In Cyprus in 1997, issues of school 'discipline' became the concern of government (Angelides, 2000), while in Denmark, a national debate about behavioural problems in schools was fuelled by media interest during 1995. This led to a government investigation in 1996 on 'behavioural disorders' in schools (Egelund and Hansen, 2000). The examples of Cyprus and Denmark highlighted the fact that the behaviour of children is always a central concern of education and that behavioural problems must always be related more to factors of 'systems' than to 'individuals'.

'Challenging' behaviour is a matter of definition and such definitions are drawn by virtue of the environments in which those behaviours take place. As Angelides suggests:

> ... the role which schools and teachers play in the development of behaviour problems is major and substantial. This perspective gives rise to the interest in schools as units, and teachers and pupils are members of those units, and not as individuals with separate unique characteristics. They are, of course, unique individuals but, at the same time, they operate as integral parts of the same institution, under the same culture, so their behaviour must be studied in relation to the specific organisational context. (Angelides, 2000, p. 57)

When a response to pupils' emotional and behavioural difficulties is sought, it is common to begin with a curiosity about the cause: 'If only we knew what caused it, we might be able to fix it ...'. In their national survey of Danish municipal schools, Egelund and Hansen (2000) identified four main themes which lay at the root of EBD. They suggest that causes of pupils' emotional and behavioural difficulties could be attributed to (on order of importance) four factors: families; teachers, instruction and school management; school and local community; and the innate characteristics of the pupils themselves. It is clear that parents are, in the first instance, considered to be the primary factor in the behaviour of their children.

Such is the nature and challenge of teaching pupils with emotional and behavioural difficulty that there have been calls for EBD to be separated from discussions of other categories of learning difficulty. In Croll and Moses' (2000) study of professional views of inclusion, one Special School head teacher is quoted as saying:

> I would like to see emotional and behavioural difficulties taken out of the special education arena. Special educational needs is really about learning difficulties. (p. 9)

Inclusive schooling of pupils with EBD raised many issues and these are highlighted by Fletcher-Campbell (2001), who identifies the issue of balance on roll as a key factor:

> Those who believed in inclusion and desired a comprehensive school nevertheless were concerned about: expenditure of time, effort and resources on a few individuals rather than on the 'normal' majority; the effect of

disruptive behaviour on the other pupils in the class or on the teacher; and the effect of gaining a reputation for success with pupils who would be at risk of exclusion elsewhere so that the intake was no longer comprehensive in socio-economic or ability terms. (Fletcher-Campbell, 2001, p. 76)

What is of concern here is that mainstream schools whose staff successfully include EBD pupils are in danger of becoming 'specialist' schools which then consequently attract more than their natural 'quota' of pupils with such difficulties. Such schools are likely to exhibit the characteristics of success, as summarised by Daniels et al. (1999), which are: good teaching; an appropriate curriculum; an effective behaviour policy; effective leadership: a core of dedicated staff; staff who are able to learn from their actions; and key members of staff who understand the nature of emotional and behavioural difficulties (Daniels et al., 1999, p. 1).

In an in-depth review of research into emotional and behavioural difficulties, Clough et al. (2004) noted that:

... those who are professionally involved in work with pupils experiencing EBD are involved, whether directly or tangentally, in their continued exclusion. ... The global movement towards inclusive practices in education has been one of the defining features of legislation by governments during the last 15 years, and has come to preoccupy the thoughts of policy makers and practitioners. International perspectives on this ... whilst illustrating its diverse contexts, practices and outcomes, have never really confronted the dilemma that the broad range of 'challenging behaviours' (including EBD) presents in moving towards a more inclusive system of educating. (p. 12)

Inclusive policies and exclusive practices

Croll and Moses' (2000) interview survey of 17 local education authority (LEA) officers and 19 head teachers in the UK (nine of whom were heads of Special Schools) points to 'widespread expressions of support for the principles of inclusion and a continuing level of support for separate special school provision' (p. 1). They identify 'support for inclusion as an ideal' but state that there is 'relatively limited influence of such an ideal on education policy'. In their survey, professionals made it clear that inclusion in mainstream classes depended on the capacity of mainstream schools to meet the needs of children with various difficulties and that this was often dependent on the 'type' and 'severity' of children's difficulties. They note that:

Inclusion as an educational ideal has the 'moral high ground', but at the day-to-day level of the thinking that informs education policy its position is much less secure. (Croll and Moses, 2000, p. 2)

A minority of participants saw inclusion as 'a real hope' (p. 11), and for them, what stood in the way of inclusion was the existing system:

> The obstacles that were placed in the way of full inclusion, and the arguments that it was unrealistic, were turned round to become a critique of the existing educational structures which presented these obstacles: a change towards inclusive policies was seen as the primary commitment from which other changes would follow. ... The criticism of educational arrangements presented by the head teachers and education officers here do not depend on a total commitment to inclusion, but can be held alongside a belief that while more children should be in mainstream schools, some children will always need separate provision. (Croll and Moses, 2000, p. 11)

Some 20 years after Italian legislation (in 1977) introduced a national policy on inclusion and eliminated state schools specifically for students 'with disabilities', Cornoldi et al. (1998) conducted a survey on the attitudes of 523 Italian teachers towards the inclusion of students with *difficolatá di apprendimento* (learning problems). While the Italian teachers expressed clear support for the concept of inclusion and a willingness to teach children with learning difficulties, they were less positive when asked if levels of support and resources were sufficient, and less than 25% thought they had sufficient skills and training. Cornoldi et al. (1998) commented:

> The majority of teachers in Italy do not receive specific university training in special education; however, some in-service training and seminars are offered. ... [The] issue of teacher training is very significant even in countries with mandated inclusion practices. (p. 354)

However, they pointed to an interesting demonstration of Italian teachers' positive attitude when they commented:

> It is clearly possible for teachers to favour the inclusion of students with disabilities in their classes without feeling that they have had sufficient training to maximise their teaching efficiency in serving these students. (p. 254)

Furthermore, they highlighted the importance, in teachers' perceptions, of sufficient assistant and support in the classroom:

> ... only 10% of Italian teachers agreed that they had sufficient personnel support. ... It may be that even Italian schools are still a long way from the amount of personnel support for inclusion that many teachers seem to consider necessary. (Cornoldi et al., 1998, p. 354)

Waldron and McLeskey (1998, p. 37) remind us of the truism that 'while inclusion may work for some children with learning disabilities some of the time, it will not work for all of these children all of the time'. But we could ask: Is it the case that segregated Special Education works for 'all of the pupils, all of the time'? Learning and development of all children – and this is particularly crucial in the early years – depends upon and is influenced by many factors; settings, teachers, environments and communities are just a few of those human factors which impact on the successful inclusion of children in mainstream settings.

Look, for example, at the approach of Denmark, a country which has pioneered many projects of integration and where the integration of pupils with various learning difficulties into mainstream classrooms has increased over the years, reflecting national policy. Attendance in pre-school education in Denmark is not compulsory, but such provision is used by 98% of preschool age children and 1.25% of primary age pupils attend special schools and classes which are for pupils with 'more serious disabilities' (Amtsrådsforeningen, 1998). Because of the high number of women in the workforce in Denmark, public preschool provision has been developed so that in 1997, the number of 2–5 year olds attending kindergarten was 86.2% (Bureau 2000/PMF_FOLA, 1997). In 2000, Egelund reported an increase in referral of Danish pupils with learning difficulties:

> The number of pupils referred to special classes and schools has increased by approximately one-third since 1990. This rise has been caused by a sharp increase in the number of children diagnosed as having severe emotional disturbance, ADHD or autism, while other categories, such as general developmental problems and speech, language and learning difficulties, have remained relatively constant. The reason for this development is not known, but it is thought to reflect developments in diagnosis, as well as the attitudes of teachers and psychologists. (Egelund, 2000, p. 93)

Karsten et al. (2001) report a longitudinal study to investigate the academic and psychosocial development of primary age pupils in mainstream and special schooling. This study seeks to evaluate the effects of the Dutch *Weer Samen Naar School* ('Back to school together again') policy which (since 1991) has sought to accommodate pupils with learning difficulties in mainstream education and so curb the growth of special schooling in the Netherlands. Few differences were found when 'at-risk' pupils in special schools and mainstream schools were compared on a range of measures. The authors argue that: 'There is little evidence to support the idea that at-risk pupils make less progress, in either their academic or psychosocial development, in regular schools compared with pupils in special schools' (p. 193).

Lipsky and Gartner (1996) reported positive effects on behavioural, social and academic development of pupils with learning difficulties while their non-disabled peers did not appear to suffer adversely from learning alongside them, and Baker, Wang and Walberg (1995, p. 34) found that 'special needs students educated in regular classes do better academically and socially than students in non-inclusive settings'. Such findings, however, are not reported in other studies which argue for the careful introduction of inclusive education (Scruggs and Mastropieri, 1996; Zigmond and Baker, 1996; Waldon and McLeskey, 1998).

In a study of primary age pupils in the Netherlands Karsten et al. (2001) found that:

> pupils in special education do less well in academic performance than pupils in regular provision. It is noticeable that the differences between special and regular education increase as the pupils get older. ... The existing lost ground is not caught up in special education and in fact the gap gets bigger as the years go by. (p. 201)

Early intervention; parents' roles; and professional development and training

We conclude our discussion of studies of inclusion of children identified as having special educational needs by drawing together some thoughts about three underpinning themes: early intervention; parents' roles; and professional development and training. These, taken with our discussion in Chapter 2 of 'rights', curriculum, developmentally appropriate practice and play, and assessment, are key in supporting the learning and development of children with learning difficulties.

Around the world, governments are developing a range of definitions and responses to the World Education Forum challenge of inclusion at the start of this new millennium. Under the Dakar Framework for Action, member countries made a commitment to vulnerable children (UNESCO, 2000) and, following this, more countries attended to their policies on special and inclusive education. This is the case, for example, in China where, as Hu et al. (2011) note:

> Inclusion of children with disabilities at the preschool level has been long overdue in China. However, inclusion is a new concept to millions of teachers, administrators and parents across the nation. In China, the term 'people with disabilities' refers to those individuals who are diagnosed by a child psychiatrist or medical doctor as having one of the following conditions: intellectual disabilities, hearing or visual impairment, physical disabilities, multiple disabilities, speech disorders and/or mental disorders. Based on the second national survey of people with disabilities in China, the government has identified 8,296,000 people with disabilities, which is 6.34% of the total population. (p. 2)

The authors, reporting on a pioneering inclusive preschool in Beijing, state that 'millions of children with special needs in China await the opportunity to grow and learn in a preschool' (Hu et al., 2011, p. 18) and that the Chinese government is aware of the 'positive societal impacts and the educational importance' (p. 18) of such provision.

Early intervention

The belief that the early years are crucial to children's later educational achievement, and to their social, emotional and physical development, has prompted the widespread development of intervention programmes, techniques and strategies which target young children who are 'at risk' in some way (Field, 2010; Allen, 2011). Such programmes are designed to make a difference to children's later educational achievement. However, it is important that those working on early intervention programmes are well equipped to do so, and appropriately qualified to understand and develop the work they do with vulnerable children and families (Jackson, 2012; Nutbrown, 2012). Early intervention programmes are based on the premise that 'beginning early' means a greater chance of being successful and are often designed to prevent difficulties as well as to seek to overcome any difficulties which young children already have.

Early intervention programmes and strategies are a response to the existence of deep inequalities in many societies and such programmes have to go further than simply providing access to early childhood education or care. Making it possible to attend some form of preschool provision often misses the most vulnerable groups, and can fail to provide the necessary support for children who are vulnerable or at risk of later school failure. The National Child Development Study (NCDS) began with data from 15,000 children all born within the same week in the UK in 1958. In the 7-year follow-up it was found that the children's teachers judged far more children whose parents were unskilled or semi-skilled manual workers to have special educational needs (24% and 17% respectively) than children whose parents were in professional groups (4% and 7%) (Davie, Butler and Goldstein, 1972). The same NCDS sample was studied at age 11. The study found that 6% of the 11 year olds were 'disadvantaged' – that is, living in single-parent or large families and in families with low income and poor housing. This 6% were some three and a half years behind their peers according to reading tests and were more likely to be receiving additional teaching support due to learning difficulties (Wedge and Prosser, 1973).

Educational disadvantage is clearly linked, with some concern to other factors, such as housing, poverty, parents' educational qualifications, and so on. The Sure Start programme in the UK can be seen as a large-scale early intervention programme which seeks to address such multiple factors which threaten children's development. Programmes like these seek to provide something specific and additional to usual main-stream provision. They are often targeted at the groups most likely to benefit and seek to change something. Many parenting programmes that are designed to support parents in managing their toddler's behaviour are early intervention programmes with the aim of bringing about a change in the child's behaviour as a result of the parent changing his or her behaviour.

Since the 1960s there have been several well-known early intervention programmes, such as the High Scope Perry Preschool Project (Schweinhart et al., 1993; Whitehurst et al., 1994; Schweinhart et al., 2004). In New Zealand, the Reading Recovery programme was designed to enhance the reading development of children, who, at around 6 years old were below their peers in terms of assessed reading attainment. Reading Recovery has since been used in many countries as a short-term programme whereby children are 'discontinued' and return to usual teaching programmes as soon as they reach an acceptable level of achievement, as assessed on a number of tests (Clay, 1972).

In a study on the inclusion of children with physical disabilities in play with their non-disabled peers in mainstream programmes, Rogow (1991) described the interventions in terms of equipment, interactions and strategies used to encourage children with physical impairments to join in group pretend play with their non-disabled peers. Rogow noted:

> Children with special needs can participate in play with peers. Social play is the arena in which social knowledge is tested and explored. Children with special needs benefit from the diverse and often demanding social experiences offered by mainstreamed programmes. Children who are fearful and uncertain may need teacher assistance to learn the intricate rules of social play, such as turn-taking or even the use of toy props. Teacher interventions in the form of modelling of pretend role play, turn taking and showing children different play possibilities highlight aspects of play interactions and show children how to play with peers. Teachers should not hesitate to talk about differences and structure play situations in which all children can participate. (1991, p. 56)

The Field Review (2012) of the effects of childhood poverty noted that:

> ... the early years (age zero to three in particular) are crucial and that interventions early in a child's life are most effective in improving outcomes and life chances. (Field, 2012, p. 90)

Further, in 2011, the Allen Review of Early Intervention set out key recommendations for early intervention, stating: 'All who care about realising the potential of our babies, children and young people need to work together and take the pathway to a long-term Early Intervention culture in the UK' (Allen, 2011, p. i). This review recommended that:

> ... the nation should be made aware of the enormous benefits to individuals, families and society of Early Intervention – a policy approach designed to build the essential social and emotional bedrock in children aged 0–3 and to ensure that children aged 0–18 can become the excellent parents of tomorrow. (p. xvii)

and

> ... the nation should recognise that influencing social and emotional capability becomes harder and more expensive the later it is attempted, and more likely to fail. (p. xvii)

and

> ... proper co-ordination of the machinery of government to put Early Intervention at the heart of departmental strategies, including those seeking to raise educational achievement and employability, improve social mobility, reduce crime, support parents and improve mental and physical health. (p. xviii)

Providing the best bespoke support, early in the lives of children, can enhance life chances, promote social mobility and reduce inequalities.

Parents' roles

The OECD (2001) report concludes that parental 'engagement' builds on parents' unique knowledge of their children and further explains:

> Parental engagement is not an attempt to teach parents to be 'involved' (they already are) or to hold them solely responsible for difficulties a child may have. In democratic ECEC institutions, the approach of professionals is to share responsibility for young children with parents, and learn from the unique knowledge that parents from diverse backgrounds can contribute. (OECD, 2001, p. 117)

We shall see later how the broad definition of inclusion reaches into much recent work in the field of parental involvement. Practitioners need to be careful to avoid and/or explain professional jargon and acronyms that might not be understood by parents (who are easily alienated by exclusive language). At the same time, practitioners must be aware of the expertise the parent may hold about their children's needs and conditions, and ensure that they consult and learn from them.

In an analysis of the terms used to communicate school policy and practice with parents, Copeland (2000) argues that there may be an 'axiomatic' exposition of SEN as a self-evident truth. He gives the following examples from school brochures:

If your child has a problem within school, this is always discussed with you. ... Mrs X is the teacher with specific responsibility for children with SEN. Mrs Y is the nominated governor with specific reference to SEN.

A further example:

The school is guided by the DfEE Code of Practice which requires us to maintain a register of children who have been identified as having SEN [in capital letters]. Parents of these children will be kept informed of their progress and the education plans which are designed to meet their needs.

Copeland (2000) comments on the 'official language' used without explanation, such as use of the SEN, and asks 'how is the reader to make sense of these statements?' Copeland suggests that:

... the concept of parents as partners is likely to become more eroded in proportion to the degree of remoteness of the expert from the school's regular personnel. (p. 247)

Most recently, policy developments in England have placed parents at the centre of early years developments, considering the need to support families as key to early years education and development (DfE, 2011).

Professional development and training

In a study of teachers' perceptions of students with EBD, Poulou and Norwich (2000) point to the need for enhanced teacher professional development. Most recently, in a review of early years qualifications, the Nutbrown Review (Nutbrown, 2012) has stressed the importance of Continued Professional Development (CPD) for all who work with young children and the importance of equality in practice and pedagogy.

A study of 141 Special Needs Coordinators in England (Crowther, Dyson and Millward, 2001) found that 72% relied on 'occasional training events' or professional development days as their only form of SEN training; none had specialist route Masters degrees and only 13% had certificate level qualifications in SEN. Emphasis in training appeared to be 'predominantly of a practical nature'. This, too, is an area that the Nutbrown Review (2012) identified as being in need of attention, highlighting that a relatively low qualified workforce did not necessarily have the training and professional development opportunities they need to properly support children and their families.

In Denmark, despite a long history of special education and of special teacher training, the law did not require education to be provided for the 'mentally retarded' until 1980, even though the first school for pupils defined by this term was set up in 1855 (Egelund, 2000). No formal edu-cational requirements exist for teachers working in special education in Denmark, although training colleges offer optional courses on 'Children with different needs'. Thus, such courses are not taken by all. Additionally, available training in special teacher education is recognised as in-service training, so does not equip newly qualified professionals (Egelund, 2000, p. 96). As professional expertise develops, Egelund suggests that roles will evolve:

> The expertise inherent in the special needs education area should be used by regular classroom teachers in the way they deal with individual differences; and special education teachers should, whenever possible, be cooperating as consultants to the regular teachers. (Egelund, 2000, p. 97)

Of teachers in the Netherlands, Karsten et al. (2001) observe that where positive developmental progress of pupils 'at risk' are observed, this strengthens the case for the professional development of teachers and the provision of support for teachers actively promoting inclusive schooling.

In two studies of practitioners' views of the inclusion of young chil-dren with special educational needs in mainstream settings, practi-tioners identified the need for professional development as crucial in enabling them to support successful inclusion and meet children's needs with confidence (Clough and Nutbrown, 2004; Nutbrown and Clough, 2004). The Nutbrown Review of qualification for the early years workforce (2012) identified the need to address ongoing profes-sional development opportunities for those who work with young children regardless of their status or role, in the interests of promoting quality provision for young children and wider understanding of equality issues.

Conclusion

In this chapter we have focused on those children for whom education is sometimes necessarily different from that offered to their peers. Children with learning difficulties are often seen as a distinct group who require specific and special attention. The issues discussed in this chapter relate specifically to the inclusion of children with SEN, but many of the enabling factors we have discussed apply equally importantly to *all* children regardless of their learning status.

In the next chapter we discuss practitioners' personal and practical definitions of inclusion.

Workshop 3 Including young children with learning difficulties

Consider Clough's (1998) suggestion that:

> In this multinational urge for inclusion lies the danger of physical inclusion but curricular and emotional exclusion unless children are included for and of themselves, by teachers who are professionally and personally equipped to provide appropriate education for all. For inclusion is about a radical deal more than physical location. (Clough, 1998, p. 5)

To what extent is there a danger that some children in your setting/service may be physically included but, due to particular learning difficulties, may be excluded from elements of curriculum, play and the setting community.

If this is the case for some children familiar to you, how might the situation be addressed so that inclusion is not just a matter of physical location but of true involvement and belonging?

Policy points

This section highlights how current policies across the four devolved administrations of the UK, while discrete, have considerable synergy of interest around the themes discussed in this chapter.

On special educational needs

In England
The DfE (2012, p. 3) outlines guiding principles which are intended to 'shape practice in early years settings'. These include a recognition that:

- Every child is a unique child, who is constantly learning and can be resilient, capable, confident and self-assured;
- Children learn and develop well in enabling environments, in which their experiences respond to their individual needs and there is a strong partnership between practitioners and parents and/or carers;
- Children develop and learn in different ways and at different rates. The framework covers the education and care of all children in early years provision, including children with special educational needs and disabilities.

In Scotland

'Children may have additional needs which require long-term support, whilst others may have shorter-term needs. How these needs impact on an individual child's development and learning varies from child to child and this determines the level and nature of support required.' (Learning and Teaching Scotland, 2010, p. 13)

And

'The curriculum must be designed, managed and delivered to take full account of each learner's individual needs and stage of development.' (Scottish Government, 2008, p. 28)

In Northern Ireland

'It is important that children have opportunities to be actively involved in practical, challenging, play-based learning in a stimulating environment, that takes account of their developmental stage/needs (including Special Educational Needs) and their own interests/experiences.' (CCEA, 2006, p. 6)

And

'Schools have a responsibility to provide a broad and balanced curriculum for all children and schools should aim to give every child the opportunity to experience success in learning and to achieve as high a standard as possible.' (CCEA, 2007, p. 2).

The document goes on to state that 'schools should give priority to the needs of the child and provide a variety of activity-based learning experiences in support of these needs' (CCEA, 2007, p. 2).

In Wales

'Practitioners must understand how children develop, and plan an appropriate curriculum that takes account of children's developmental needs and the skills that they need to grow to become confident learners.' (Welsh Assembly Government, 2008, p. 5)

The inclusion of children with learning difficulties

In England

'Reasonable adjustments to the assessment process for children with special educational needs and disabilities must be made as appropriate. Providers should consider whether they may need to seek specialist assistance to help with this. Children will have differing levels of skills and abilities across the Profile and it is important that there is a full assessment of all areas of their development, to inform plans for future activities and to identify any additional support needs.' (DfE, 2012, p. 12)

In Scotland

'Children have different dispositions and preferences and there are natural differences in the ways in which they learn as well as the pace of learning. Effective staff pay close attention ...' (Learning and Teaching Scotland, 2010, p. 23)

And the Scottish Government (2008, p.7) recognises that there should be:

- 'A coherent and inclusive curriculum from 3 to 18 wherever learning is taking place, whether in schools, colleges or other settings';
- 'More opportunities to develop skills for learning, skills for life and skills for work for all young people at every stage';
- 'Appropriate pace and challenge for every child'.

In Northern Ireland

It is recommended that plans for learning and development should 'provide for the needs of individual children' and that 'positive learning environments [are those] suitable for the developmental stage of the children.' (CCEA, 2006, p. 8)

And that

'Schools have a responsibility to provide a broad and balanced curriculum for all children and should aim to give every pupil the opportunity to experience success in learning and to achieve as high a standard as possible ... teachers will be aware that pupils have different experiences, interests and strengths.' (CCEA, 2007, p. 3)

In Wales

'A curriculum for young children should be appropriate to their stage of learning rather than focusing solely on age-related outcomes to be achieved. Children should move on to the next stages of their learning when they are developmentally ready and at their own pace.' (Welsh Assembly Government, 2008, p. 4)

Further reading

Garner, P. (2009) *Special Educational Needs: The Key Concepts*. London: Routledge.
Wall, K. (2010) *Special Needs and Early Years: A Practitioner Guide*. London: Sage.

Defining inclusion

Introduction

In this chapter we report on our study of the personal practices, beliefs and values around inclusive issues held by early childhood educators working in a range of policy contexts in the UK. Differing policies within the UK's constituent countries – England, Northern Ireland, Scotland and Wales – are borne out of cultural, historical and political identities and, at the same time, influenced (to varying degrees) by early childhood practices and policies in other European countries. More or less distinctive beliefs about childhood and about the aims and purposes for early education can be identified in various policies.

In these policy contexts, 452 early childhood educators from around the UK participated in a study which aimed to understand something of the ways in which policies impacted on personal practices. Building on earlier work (Clough and Nutbrown, 2003, 2004; Nutbrown and Clough, 2004), the study reported in this chapter had two aims: first, to identify practitioners' *definitions* of 'inclusion' and, secondly, to uncover something of practitioners' *beliefs about* inclusion through their own personal accounts and stories. The chapter uses the words of practitioners to illustrate their views about: the 'rightness' of inclusion; the importance of finding ways to talk about difficult issues, and the personal willingness of practitioners to seek inclusion as a first option.

Policy contexts in the UK

Two broad aspects of policy are important here: generic early years policy and specific policy related to inclusive societies and schooling. As we have seen earlier, policy developments across the UK have, in recent years, changed the landscape of early childhood education and care in terms of curriculum and pedagogy and, similarly, systems and services.

Early childhood education and care policies across the UK of the 1990s and 2000s brought radical change to curriculum and pedagogy, and to state-funded systems and services, and the pace of change in the 2010s has continued. Important strides in policy development have been made in all four countries in the UK and the following initiatives are characteristic of a general tenor and scope typical of the last decade:

- *Sure Start* (DES/DWP, 2003) represents investment on an unprecedented scale and multi-agency innovation in community-based early years provision across the UK.
- The Children Act 2004 (DfES, 2004), which we have already discussed.
- The *Review of Preschool Education* in Northern Ireland (DENI, 2004) is an indication of how curriculum can be developed to support the fulfilment of key aims for a society.
- The *Early Years Foundation Stage* 0–5 has established a programme of learning for children in the first stage of education in England (DfE, 2012).
- The *Foundation Phase* 3–7 in Wales (The Welsh Assembly 2004, 2008) shows how a country can draw in various experiences across the world, first to redefine 'the early years', and secondly to propose a system of early education which is designed to enable all children to reach their potential and limit the possibility of creating educational failure.
- In Scotland (Scottish Executive, 2003) new approaches to assessment have been informed by a view of early education curriculum which is informal, individualistic and diverse. This was followed by *A Framework for Learning and Teaching* (The Scottish Government, 2008) and policy, *Pre-Birth to Three* (Learning and Teaching Scotland, 2010).

This nation-wide interest in early childhood provision is paralleled with similar far-reaching changes in inclusive policies. The success of Sure Start, an essentially inclusive policy realised in practice nation-wide, can be attributed to three embedded principles:

1 Its locally and community defined projects (within national targets).
2 The multi-agency focus on marginalised and disadvantaged communities where educational achievement is low and young children and their families experience multiple difficulties.
3 Provision of an unprecedented level of funding to support this ambitious policy development.

Nationally and (perhaps more importantly) within local communities, Sure Start brought together existing initiatives and developed new projects to address a range of issues, such as: poverty; housing; ill-health; smoking, drug and alcohol addiction; teenage pregnancy and parenting skills (Weinberger et al., 2005). Social factors such as these dominate the lives of many families in marginalised communities and can, if they are not addressed appropriately, make for exclusion as well as the increasing concentration of families with multiple needs in the communities in which they live.

As we discussed in the previous chapter, The Children Act 2004 sought to create: 'A legislative framework for: improving outcomes for all children; to protect them; to promote their well-being; to support all children to develop their full potential' (*Every Child Matters* (Green Paper), 2003). With the emphasis on *all* children, the Children Act 2004 could be seen as an attempt towards inclusive responses to protection of and provision for children. The Act seeks to address 'causes' and to reduce the number of young children 'in need'. Initiatives promoted in *Every Child Matters* included: Sure Start Children's Centres ('one stop' nursery education, family support, employment advice, childcare, health services); full-service extended schools (pre- and post-school care); speech and language therapy; homelessness support and housing advice; support for parents and carers; early intervention and effective provision; accountability and integration (locally, regionally, nationally); workforce reform to bring about flexibility in working and appropriate qualification and remuneration.

The early years of the 2000s saw early childhood education across the whole of the UK as the focus of increased, perhaps intensive, recognition. Policy makers in all four countries of the UK were speaking with increasing frequency and volubility of young children and their needs, of the importance of multi-agency, 'joined-up' services, of parenting support and the importance of early education and care provision. Heightened political recognition and a consubstantial increase in funding was responsible for the expansion of provision, the development of services and a reshaping of the activities in early childhood settings. The aim was to provide targeted services which met, without stigmatising, the needs of a diverse range of families and assisted in encouraging women into the workforce (and out of poverty) by providing education and care for their young children. The economic downturn since 2008 has hit services hard and the growth in provision and services has slowed. As a result, many opportunities for the expansion of provision have been curtailed as local authorities have had to reduce their salary bills, thus cutting jobs and, with them, the professional and support services they provided. The study reported in the next section, therefore, took place in a very different policy context from that of the UK in 2012. This shift may, not necessarily through deliberate policy moves but by virtue of the economic and political context of the times, force a redefinition of inclusion, for there are dangers that more families will become excluded as the economic climate worsens. More families are in danger of becoming homeless, and with that come difficulties in relationships, health, employment, and so on.

The study: origins, aims and methodology

In varied and, predominantly, *pro*-inclusive UK policy contexts 452 early childhood educators participated in a UK-wide study, giving their personal responses to policies and identifying the ways in which such policies impacted on their practice. The study built on earlier work (Clough and Nutbrown 2004; Nutbrown and Clough, 2004), which surveyed practitioners' beliefs and practices around inclusion. Early childhood educators working in a range of (non-specialist) settings and services participated in the study reported in this chapter. These included: voluntary preschool groups, independent day nurseries, independent schools, Steiner-Waldorf kindergartens, Montessori nursery schools, Foundation Stage nursery and reception classes. All participants had regular, daily contact with children and worked in settings which served families from a range of cultural, religious and social groups. They were first asked to generate and then to discuss definitions of the term 'inclusion'.

A variety of methods of data collection was used, including email dialogue, questionnaire, face-to-face interviews, telephone interviews, taped focus group discussions, open-ended written reactions to statements read to them (or presented on PowerPoint). Taken together, and analysed using a computer-assisted analysis package (NVivo), these data provide a rich insight into practitioners' definitions of inclusion.

Practitioners' personal definitions of inclusion

We asked 182 practitioners (drawn from the larger sample) from a range of settings and services to develop and agree (in groups of five or six), a definition of inclusion which they felt could be applied to their own early childhood setting. In all, 34 group definitions were generated and these fell into an almost even split between two main categories: 15 could be classified as 'narrow' definitions and the remaining 19 were classified as 'broad' definitions of inclusion. Fifteen groups (a total of 96 participants) created 'narrow' definitions which defined 'inclusion' as an issue relating to children with special educational needs or learning difficulties. Typical examples of such definitions included:

> Inclusion is treating every child as an individual (regardless of their difficulty) and seeking knowledge and understanding from outside organisations,

e.g. courses that are available, and we need guidance on an individual basis. Ideally, we could use continued support so that we can continue to meet the needs of each child with learning difficulties.

Inclusion is right for most children but not all. Some children's needs are so specific that catering for them in a mainstream setting would be difficult. Inclusion is ideal when both parents and practitioners are fully aware of the disabled child's needs and are able to provide the support and resources to meet these needs. The needs of the child are paramount – whatever the policy.

Nineteen groups (a total of 86 practitioners) developed 'broad' definitions of inclusion which identified the importance of including many more potentially excluded or marginalised groups. Typical examples in this 'broad' inclusion category were:

Successful inclusion promotes positive relationships with all children and parents, within an environment where children's individuality is celebrated – whatever children's backgrounds or learning needs. Staff expertise, sensitivity and professional attitude develop children's learning, ensuring that all children are happy, empowered and are given the opportunity to reach their full potential and be proud of themselves.

Inclusion is striving to include all children within a setting which celebrates the differences in all children – with the help, support and guidance of the child, parents and other professionals. We should meet the needs of each individual child and enable them to fulfil their potential in all areas of learning. Inclusion takes account of children's family heritage as well as specific difficulties.

For us, inclusion is accepting each child as an individual. This applies to travelling children, refugees, families in poverty, families from minority religious and cultural groups as well as children with learning difficulties. Inclusion means ensuring everyone works together in the child's best interests to enable them to reach their full potential – EVERYONE!

These 'narrow' and 'broad' definitions of inclusion are reflected in much of the literature, some of which continues to portray inclusion as treating fairly, exclusively of disability and learning difficulties, while others seek to open out the definition of 'inclusion' to incorporate all potentially excluded groups and individuals. Early years curriculum policies, however, make specific mention of children with learning difficulties, for example:

Practitioners will need to plan for each child's individual learning requirements, including those children who need additional support or have particular needs or disabilities. The focus should be on removing barriers for children where these already exist and on preventing learning difficulties from developing. Early years practitioners have a key role to play in working with parents to identify learning needs and respond quickly to any area of particular difficulty, and to develop an effective strategy to meet these needs, making good use of individual educational plans, so that later difficulties can be avoided. (QCA/DfES, 2008b, p. 18)

At the same time, though, they strongly promote 'broadly' inclusive practices, thus:

... no child should be excluded or disadvantaged because of ethnicity, culture or religion, home language, family background, special educational needs, disability, gender or ability. (QCA/DfES, 2008b, p. 11)

This latter, 'broad view' of inclusion is promoted by the Centre for Studies in Inclusive Education (CSIE) which argues that:

Regular schools with this inclusive orientation are the most effective means of combating discriminatory attitudes, creating welcoming communities, building on an inclusive society and achieving education for all; moreover, they provide an effective education to the majority of children and improve the efficiency and ultimately the cost-effectiveness of the entire education system. (CSIE, 1995, p. 8)

Indeed, some seek to emphasise the merely *contingent* association of 'special educational needs' and impairment with inclusive education. As Booth has it:

Some continue to want to make inclusion primarily about 'special needs education' or the inclusion in education of children and young people with impairments but that position seems absurd. ... If inclusion is about the development of comprehensive community education and about prioritising community over individualism beyond education, then the history of inclusion is the history of these struggles for an education system which serves the interests of communities and which does not exclude anyone within those communities. (Booth, 2000, p. 64)

As provision for education and care for children of all ages establishes ways of meeting education targets together with wider social challenges the 'broad' view of inclusion seems to be gaining currency. Lingard (2000) similarly emphasises the larger structures of inclusion in diversity:

What I want to do is to hold to a broader definition which links across the whole social justice, equity and citizenship issues. The concept of inclusion might also encourage an across-government approach to social and economic disadvantage. (p. 101)

The practitioners in our study who developed and discussed 'narrow' and 'broad' definitions of inclusion reflect a spectrum of understanding about what inclusion *means*. Their understandings vary from the view that it is 'only' the latest 'politically correct' term for 'Special Educational Needs' to the view that it is an all-embracing, anti-discriminatory practice which makes *all* users and participants in any provision equally valued members of a community where all 'belong'.

Responses to inclusive policies

We asked participants to respond to the following three statements about inclusion and exclusion:

> There's too much segregation in society ... young children should learn about differences and – before prejudices are formed – they can experience living together with others who are different. (Teacher, Northern Ireland)

> No, some children cannot tolerate the presence of their peers and become very distressed. (Playleader, Scotland)

> Some children should not be included because they could create an uncomfortable environment. (Anonymous)

These statements triggered important and passionate moral arguments about 'inclusion', 'respect' and 'rights' on the one hand, and practicalities, 'survival' of practitioners and funding on the other. Often practitioners stood effectively in both camps, expressing what was 'right' along with the caveat of what was 'possible' in their present contexts. Elsewhere we have noted the reservations which practitioners often build into their constructions of inclusion as a sort of '*Yes ... but...*' factor (Clough and Nutbrown, 2004; Nutbrown and Clough, 2004). The following discussion is an example of this:

> *Mary*: I think the first teacher is right. Letting children mix together before they understand about differences and develop prejudices – that's right. But it's not so easy as that – there are barriers to overcome – in the community. Not everyone ...
>
> *Aisha*: Some parents wouldn't like to think that their children might miss out – I mean – especially if a child with disruptive behaviour was in the group. It's ...
>
> *Mary*: Exactly – and it's not fair to the others.
>
> *Jo*: But you can't just say 'we can't have you you're too difficult to cope with!' It's, it's – well – immoral!
>
> *Aisha*: It's being realistic though – you get too many being disruptive and the quiet ones miss out. Especially quiet little girls.

Mary: I believe in equality – I believe …

Jo: Equality means giving everyone – all of them – an equal chance!

Aisha: Not necessarily in the same provision though. Equality – yeah – but … but not at any price, not at any cost to the whole group.

Mary: It should be a first option – we should always try to include …

Jo: Easier said than done – but yes – I think Mary's right.

Aisha: You wouldn't say that if you worked where I work!

As others have shown (Angelides, 2000; Croll and Moses, 2000; Clough et al., 2004), such qualified commitment to inclusion is arguably most apparent in the case of children with Emotional and Behavioural Difficulties (EBD), which presents educators with more difficulties than does the inclusion of children with, say, physical impairment. Visser et al. (2003) remind us that children with EBD are no less to be considered as part of our community and that:

> schools need to be communities which are open, positive, and diverse, not selective, exclusive or rejecting. They need to be 'barrier free' for pupils with EBD. The development of a collaborative ethos is a key feature. … Schools need to develop a sense of equity in promoting every pupil's rights and responsibilities in all aspects of school life. These lessons are easy to state but we know … just how difficult it is for schools to achieve the challenges they pose. (p. 45)

In the study reported in this chapter, we have noted that personal willingness on the part of practitioners to include children and their families seemed, for some, to be matched with despair and lack of support or knowledge or confidence in their own abilities and, in some cases, in systems and structures which were not supporting inclusive policies. While many practitioners began their discussions by identifying with a relatively narrow view of inclusion, many – in conversation with others and with us – moved their positions to consider a broader view of inclusion as they identified the mis-match between what they believed should happen and what was often their experience, the latter being dependent upon available resources and enabling structures. The general consensus seemed to be that inclusion was the 'right' thing for young children and that the challenge was to create environments and systems where all had a place.

This chapter has highlighted some personal definitions of inclusion in the context of early childhood education and care. It has drawn on the voices of practitioners who have demonstrated that the term *inclusion* means different things to different people and that *acts of inclusion* vary from setting to setting. In the following chapter, we show how some practitioners who participated in our study confronted various scenarios of inclusion in a context where the challenge was to *think* inclusively.

Workshop 4 Defining inclusion

In our study we used the following exercise as one means of gathering data on definitions of inclusion. Staff teams may find it useful to try this as a starting point for their own work to define what inclusion means to them.

1 Working alone, write down your own definition of inclusion.
2 Swap your definition with a colleague.
3 Question each other about what your definition actually means. Can you defend it? Do you want to change anything?
4 Make any changes to your definition if you wish to do so.
5 Work in groups of about four. Share your definitions and try to develop a shared and agreed definition for your group.
6 Close the session by sharing the group definitions with the whole team.

Follow-up

After the session, type up individual and group definitions (anonymously if you wish). Use these definitions as a basis for further discussion within the team at a second session. The aim here is to find common ground, understand differences and reach a point where the whole team can come to an understanding and agreed definition of inclusion for the setting.

Colleagues may find it useful to refer to their notes from Workshops 1 and 2 in their discussion.

Policy points

Across the UK policies supporting inclusive practices vary.

Inclusion

In England
Inclusion is about ...

... practitioners responding 'to each child's emerging needs and interests, guiding their development through warm, positive inter-action.' (DfE, 2012, p. 6)

... 'provision for children who wish to relax, play quietly or sleep, equipped with appropriate furniture.' (DfE, 2012, p. 24)

... practitioners developing targeted plans to support a child's future learning and development if there are 'significant emerging concerns, or an identified special educational need or disability' or areas 'where the child's progress is less than expected.' (DfE, 2012, p. 24)

... 'quality and consistency in all early years settings, so that every child makes good progress and no child gets left behind.' (DfE, 2012, p. 12)

... practitioners considering 'the individual needs, interests, and stage of development of each child in their care and [using] this information to plan a challenging and enjoyable experience for each child in all of the areas of learning and development.' (DfE, 2012, p. 6)

And

... paying close attention to children. If there is any 'cause for concern, practitioners must discuss this with the child's parents and/or carers and agree how to support the child.' (DfE, 2012, p. 6)

In Scotland
Policy relating to inclusion in Scotland states that:

'Inclusion and responsive care are crucial if children's rights are to be promoted effectively. Through working closely with parents and other professionals, staff in early years settings recognise that all those involved with children and families have an important contribution to make.' (Learning and Teaching Scotland, 2010, p. 20)

'Taking meaningful account of the four key principles of the Rights of the Child, Relationships, Responsive Care and Respect should ensure that staff help families to achieve the best possible start for all children.' (Learning and Teaching Scotland, 2010, p.47)

'Supporting children and young people in their learning involves a range of people – parents and carers, nursery teachers and nurses, primary teachers, secondary teachers, support staff, college staff, psychological services, Skills Development Scotland, volunteers and workers from voluntary organisations and local authority youth work provision. It is important to work in partnership to "get it right for every child".' (Scottish Government, 2008, p. 21)

In Northern Ireland

'Learning is supported by adults when early years practitioners are committed, sensitive, enthusiastic and interact effectively.' (CCEA, 2006, p. 4)

'Relationships are strengthened through shared enjoyment and respect, where adults working with young children respond positively with warmth, genuine praise and encouragement. It is also important that adults are sincere, fair and honest with children, patient, allowing time for children to adjust to the setting [are] consistent and have a positive approach to behaviour management.' (CCEA, 2006, p. 7)

'A multi-professional approach exists and practitioners access the expertise of other professionals.' (CCEA, 2006, p. 4)

'Teachers have flexibility to interpret the programmes to suit the needs, interests and abilities of the children.' (CCEA, 2006, p. 9)

'In planning curriculum and assessment activities, teachers should be aware of the requirements of the equal opportunities legislation and the Special Educational Needs and Disability Order (SENDO) and should have high expectations for all pupils, including pupils with special educational needs, pupils with disabilities, pupils from all social and cultural backgrounds, pupils of different ethnic groups including travellers and those from diverse linguistic backgrounds.' (CCEA, 2007, p. 3)

In Wales

'Practitioners must understand how children develop, and plan an appropriate curriculum that takes account of children's developmental needs and the skills that they need to grow to become confident learners. Account also needs to be taken of barriers to play, to learning and participation caused by physical, sensory, communication or learning difficulties. The experiences that children have had before entering the setting/school need to be recognised and considered.' (Welsh Assembly Government, 2008, p. 5)

Further reading 📖

Connolly, P. (2004) *Boys and Schooling in the Early Years*. London: Routledge Falmer.

Gussin Paley, V. (1984) *Boys and Girls: Superheroes in the Doll Corner*. Chicago, IL, and London: University of Chicago Press.

Holland, P. (1999) Is 'zero-tolerance' intolerance? An under-fives centre takes a fresh look at their policy on war/weapons/superhero practice. *Early Childhood Practice*, 1(1): 24–45.

5

Thinking Inclusion

Introduction

So far in this book we have discussed research studies relating to inclusion, considered the specific issues that concern children identified as having special educational needs, and presented, from our own research, a range of definitions of inclusion as they have been developed by practitioners from around the UK and other parts of Europe. In this chapter we demonstrate how practitioners can develop their practice of *thinking inclusion* when they are asked to consider a series of scenarios in which inclusive issues are raised. We present role-play scripts and stories which were created by some of the practitioners in our study and others we have worked with recently. We originally used a total of eight scenarios (based on real situations) as a method of data collection on the practices of practitioners faced with such situations. In each case practitioners role-played, or wrote an account, to demonstrate how issues of inclusion and exclusion might be addressed as they worked with parents and 'the system' to ensure that the learning and development needs of the children were met. In this chapter we have included four such scenarios which focus on different arenas of inclusion and exclusion; in each case we first present the scenario that we gave to the practitioners, followed by their creative responses to what they were given.

Scenario 1   George

George has Autism. He is three and a half years old. He lives with his mother, a single parent, who wants him to attend the nursery in his local

(Continued)

(Continued)

primary school. A meeting is held at the school where George's mother, the nursery teacher and the Special Needs support teacher for the area meet to explore the possibility of George attending the nursery.

Develop a short role-play with at least three characters:

- George's mother
- The nursery teacher
- The Special Needs support worker

In the role-play:

- George's mother should describe his needs and characteristics
- The nursery teacher should explain why/why not George can attend
- The Special Needs teacher should attempt to meet any specific needs

What happens?

The role-play

Nursery Teacher (NT):	Hello Mrs Grainger. Come on in and have a seat. Do you want a coffee or tea or anything?
Mrs G:	No I just I've just had some.
NT:	I don't know if you've met Sally Cuthbert [*SC*], have you? Sally's going to be George's support worker.
Mrs G:	I had the letter from you, didn't I?
SC:	That's right. It's nice to meet you at last. Thanks for coming in...
Mrs G:	Can I just ask before..., I mean, is it going to be all right for George, I mean, coming here?
NT:	Well, we need to talk about what George needs, what's best for George – it might be that Meltham House would be better...
Mrs G:	He's not going there, he's just not! He's only 3, just a baby, really... and he needs a chance. What happened at Playgroup was a mistake, they just didn't understand, they...
SC:	Sorry? What did happen at Playgroup? Which Playgroup was that?
Mrs G:	He went to Scallywags.
SC:	On Dent Road?
Mrs G:	Yeah.
SC:	Mmm... when was that?
Mrs G:	That was, ooh 6, 7 months ago, but he didn't go for long, I mean, I wouldn't let him after what happened.

[*Mrs G is clearly getting upset and is on the verge of tears*]

NT: Here [*offering tissues*] don't worry, please... we...

Mrs G: It was just dreadful, it was dreadful for him. He was so unhappy, I knew he was but they just saw him as a sort of nuisance, a yob or something. They didn't understand that he needed routine, needed regular faces and, well, that place, I don't know... perhaps they just work on endless part-timers or something, but George hardly ever saw the same teacher twice in a week – all the time he was there. And the greeting routine in the morning... well, it wasn't a routine. It was whoever was at the gate or the door or whatever, and they'd do it differently. Some wanted to take his hand, which was nice and everything, but he doesn't like that. And there was one woman who always asked him to take his coat off straight away and, well, George takes his coat off when George's ready, y'know? And there was one day when the welcomer was wearing a yellow t-shirt and he just went – George just went bonkers, absolutely bonkers. And it was worse when we went in. Everything was... it was Yellow Day or something, and they'd all got yellow table cloths and yellow, well, yellow everything, y'know? And the one, Jenny, who George really started to like and, well, she came over and she says: come with me, George, it's Yellow Day we're going to have fun today and he just lay on the floor, just lay down and curled up, like in a little ball, and just whined. He whined and whined like he does when he can't, well, he just can't handle. Y'know he was such a lovely little boy [*Mrs Grainger has started to weep again*], such an ordinary, lovely little boy 'til he was about 2, or nearly 2, always chattering like a little bird – my mum used to call him Christopher Robin – he was so sunny, y'know?

SC: So, the playgroup didn't know about George's specific preferences – didn't know he hated yellow, for example?

Mrs G: Right, and there was the toilet thing too. He hated the smell, so when they said 'toilet time' he would squeal and refuse to go – weed himself sometimes – but he couldn't help it. I don't think they understood. They weren't unkind – just didn't seem to know and didn't really get it that he was different. They were good to him, though, gave him a place, they tried... but I, I , well – y'know? I guess I could have helped more – told them stuff – I just wanted him to fit in – didn't want to draw attention...

NT: I think we can learn from this. I know it's been upsetting for you, but I think if we get as much information from you as possible – really build up a picture of George – I think we can do something? What do you think, Sally?

SC: He needs routine, yes? And stability of staffing? And you know the things that really upset him, yes – I think we can – try certainly. We'll need your help, Mrs Grainger, to make sure we get it right for him. Well, as best we can! We'll make sure all the staff know what you tell us – if that's OK – and set up a shared record book that he brings home each day and we all write in – good stuff and the not so good? That takes a bit of effort from everyone to make sure important bits are written down, but it is a way of making sure we all know. You can say if he's had a bad night, we can say what he's done at nursery.

Mrs G: And you won't do Yellow Day!

NT: [*Laughing*] Well, if we do plan anything that we think will upset George we'll tell you in good time so that some sort of alternative arrangement can be sorted out for him! How about that?

SC: OK, so could we meet so that I can do a really detailed history of George? I could come to your home if that suits you – and meet George too, see him with his own things – find out what he likes and what disturbs him?

Mrs G: Yes, that's fine. Sounds helpful, so long as you're not checking up on me. Since his Dad left I...

NT: Oh, no, no – no way. There's nothing like that. We just want to do all we can to help get things as good as we can for George.

SC: Definitely! Is that OK? Now [*looking in her diary*] how about next Wednesday morning?

Mrs G: That's fine – as soon as you can...

NT: Is there anything else for now, Mrs Grainger? Anything at all?

Mrs G: Do you think you'll be able to let him come here? Give him a chance? I mean – what if he doesn't pass...

SC: Mrs Grainger, it's not about 'passing'. I'm coming to see you to try to work out how best we can meet George's needs.

NT: We'll give him a chance, Mrs Grainger, we'll do our best, and see how it goes? OK?

Mrs G: [*Getting up*] Thank you, thanks so much. I'll do everything – anything – you know....

        [*SC, NT and Mrs G shake hands and Mrs G leaves...*]

SC: [*Turning to NT*] Poor woman – all that on her own. I really think talking with her, getting the detail... I think your team will be able to provide for George.

NT: Hope so, we'll give it our best shot!

Scenario 2 Mary

Mary is four and a half years old. She is the middle child of five in a travelling family (there is a 6 week-old baby boy, a 3 year-old girl and two older boys aged 6 and 9). The family have been living at the local Travellers' site for about three months. Mary has a place in the reception class at the nearby primary school. She rarely attends and the head teacher has written three letters to the family and visited their trailer twice. She finds the father 'obstructive, abusive and uncooperative' and has referred Mary's case to Social Services, via the social worker attached to the school.

A meeting is held in the local community rooms, because the father has refused to attend a meeting at the school.

Develop a short role-play with at least three characters:

- Mary's father
- The head teacher
- The local community social worker (traveller support)

In the role-play:

- Mary's father should describe Mary's needs and characteristics and why he thinks the Reception class isn't helping her.
- The head teacher should explain what the school can and cannot do.
- The social worker should seek to identify anything that Social Services can do to help.

What happens?

The role-play

The role-play begins with Jane Higgins, the local community social worker, buying tea from the coffee bar in the community rooms. Chairs and tables are scattered around and a few others are sitting in armchairs talking. Sarah Ash, the head teacher, is sitting at a table, sorting out some papers in her diary. There is no sign of Mr Donnolly. Jane returns to Sarah with their tea. She glances at her watch. It is 2.20 pm and the meeting was arranged for 2.00 pm.

Sarah Ash:	I never expected him to turn up. He's no intention of cooperating with us in any way.
Jane Higgins:	Something might have happened – give him the benefit of the doubt. You never know, maybe he got held up. Anyway, do you see any solutions to this? Have you had any thoughts on what we might do to help?
SA:	Mary should be coming to school. She's missing out on so much and surely it would help her mother if she was out of that trailer during the day. It can't be easy with a young baby.
JH:	There's the traveller support service – the education team – what have they offered? I couldn't get hold of anyone yesterday.
SA:	They say the family is on their list for a visit... [*Mr Donnolly enters. He's heard part of the conversation as he walks in. JH gets up and makes towards him.*]
JH:	Ah! Mr Donnolly – we were just...
Mr D:	Talking about us – I 'erd ya.
JH:	Just thinking about how we might be able to help...
Mr D:	Who said we needed 'elp? Eh? I din't say we wanted no 'elp.
JH:	Mr Donnelly, would you like some tea or coffee?
Mr D:	Nah! Let's get on wiv it – wot d'u want any'ow?
SA:	Well, we – I – we're very worried that Mary is missing so much of school. It's seriously delaying her learning – she's struggling with reading and...
Mr D:	She's a babby – she's 4 year old. Readin? Come off it! There's time enough. I din't read till I was 10 or so.
SA:	And she's not getting the opportunity to socialise with other children... She's not integrating with her peers...
Mr D:	Fancy words Mrs. ... She does plenty of that socialisin' stuff – loads of kids on the site – and she's talkin', no trouble with 'er talkin'.
JH:	Mr Donnolly, wouldn't it help your wife if Mary came to school? With the baby and all that?
Mr D:	She's got enough on her – wot wiv the babby. She can't see to Mary too, with the uniform and that, and bringing her up 'ere – all very well but you try it – she's got enough on!

JH: How would your wife feel if the travelling support service helped with getting Mary to school? Picked her up in the morning?

Mr D: I don't want no one snoopin' round us – we look after our kids.

JH: No, not snooping, just calling at a time we agree in the morning to pick her up and take her to school, give your wife time to sort out the baby so that she doesn't have to come out with the baby every morning. Might that help?

Mr D: I'd 'av ta ask 'er like. We don't need 'elp ta look afta us kids like...

JH: No, but just at the moment maybe helping with getting Mary to school? Just for a week or two, until some sort of routine gets sorted?

SA: It would really help her if she came to school on a regular basis.

        [*Mr Donnolly sneers at Sarah Ash. He has taken a dislike to her – her tone and vocabulary appear to repel him. He turns his back slightly, rebuffing her, but has seemed to warm to Jane Higgins. He looks at her and speaks.*]

Mr D: Well, at last someone talkin' sense instead of all that highfollutin' education jargon. See wot you can do, deary, and if you can do that – get her to school – then I'll see what Mrs Donnolly has to say. I'm not promisin' though. Mary's bright as a button – learning loads.

        [*Mr D gets up to leave. Jane Higgins gets up as well and walks with him to the door. Sarah Ash stands by the table.*]

JH: Mr Donnolly, I'll see what can be sorted out and I'll call at the site to let you know. Sarah Ash really does want the best for Mary, you know. She...

Mr D: Yeah! Big words! Mary will read soon enough. But thank you, deary – see what you can do. It'll 'elp 'er mum if she's outta the 'van in the mornings.

        [*Mr Donnolly leaves. Jane Higgins returns to finish her tea and says...*]

JH: Sarah, he's just frightened of authority. That's why he's having a go at your language. I'll see what Traveller Education can do and we'll do our best to sort it out.

The scene ends with the two women finishing their tea in silence. Jane Higgins is dialling a number on her mobile phone.

Scenario 3   Ahmed

Ahmed is 4 years old. He lives with his family on a poor inner-city housing estate. The family have been granted asylum and are now living in local authority housing, away from any relatives or other members of the wider Pakistani Muslim community. Ahmed's older brother and sister attend the local comprehensive school. His father has found some work as a night porter at the hospital five miles away and works long hours. His mother speaks no English, though her older children are teaching her. Ahmed has been attending the local nursery in the mornings for the last six weeks. He is the only Pakistani Muslim child in the school and there is no specific support for him. He cries most of the time. When he didn't attend, the next day the nursery nurse went to the home to see if anything was wrong (non-attendance was a regular occurrence at this nursery and so this was usual practice). She arrived to find the mother scrubbing paint and faeces off the front door and windows. Racist taunts were daubed on the concrete wall at the side of the house. She thinks that this is not the first time this has happened.

A meeting takes place at the school.

- Ahmed's mother (and her 15 year-old son as translator) attend – they don't understand what's going on but they are worried that Ahmed is continually crying.
- The head teacher attends – she is trying to find a solution to help Ahmed and thinks it might help if the mother stays with him in the nursery.
- The local community liaison officer attends – he is keen to find out the extent of the abuse to the family.

What happens?

The account

Written by a small group of practitioners in response to Scenario 3.

Although we were very disturbed by this – it's something we recognised from the media – none of us (the people in our group) has had such a thing happen to families in our settings. But we know this sort of racist behaviour goes on. What would we do?

We think this is a re-housing issue. It's not a case of not trying to include the child in the nursery – we could try that – get some bilingual support – invite the mother to come with him until he is settled – make use of older siblings who can speak English. And it could be that that would have to be done, but the major task is something bigger than the nursery can handle. We think that in this case it's a broader issue of inclusion. It would seem cruel – we feel – to try to focus on including the child in the nursery when the real problem is that this family is not included in wider society. In this particular poor, white, run down community there is so much racial prejudice – in fact, prejudice against anyone who is different from them. Anyone with a decent car or a job or who does not speak in the distinctive local slang is treated with suspicion.

We imagine – in this neglected community where everyone is struggling – we imagine that there will be resentment that they have a council house and that the father has a job and that the child has a nursery place. There will be a sense that this refugee family have arrived and been 'given everything'.

We may not be right on this, but there's so much distress in this family – they are all coping with the trauma of leaving their own home and country and of trying to settle into a very different life. So, we think we would try to put pressure on the local authority to re-house the family nearer to the wider Pakistani Muslim community. There's a danger with this – that all minority ethnic groups are 'put' together – and therefore, in the long term, there's less integration in society as a whole, but we're thinking how awful it is for them all just now. The poor mother cleaning faeces off the windows, poor little traumatised Ahmed, and the older children having the responsibility of translating everything and being involved in some very difficult discussions, knowing things that perhaps – if they weren't translating – they would not know. So, in the bigger picture, there's work to do around building more cohesion, tolerance, acceptance and community among different ethnic groups, but for this family – they've been through so much – that we'd go for re-housing as the aim.

Scenario 4   James, Chris and Ellie

Ellie is 2 years old. She attends a nursery each morning, being dropped off by James at around 8 am as he is on his way to work. Chris, having worked part-time since they adopted Ellie, picks her up just after 1 pm in the after-noon. Ellie loves coming to nursery, she has settled well and seems to have developed close relationships with children and adults in the setting. She is part of a loving family and her parents, who clearly adore her, have enjoyed being part of the life of the nursery, attending parents' events, outings and workshops about various aspects of young children's learning and development.

Everything was fine until one afternoon, when Chris walked into the nursery to collect Ellie, a father was clearly heard to be abusive to him,

(Continued)

(Continued)

saying that Chris and his partner 'disgusted' him and other parents and that they should not be allowed to look after a little girl – 'they couldn't be trusted'. This was followed by a tirade of anti-gay taunts and abuse which was heard by staff and children before the caretaker came and informed him that if he did not stop and leave immediately he would call the police. Chris was visibly shaken at this attack and went immediately to Ellie's key person to tell her what had happened.

By the time James got home that night, Chris was outraged, and wondering what else he should do. He had received several phone calls from parents who had heard about the incident and wanted to express their support. Chris was now wondering what effect this form of abusive, homophobic behaviour might ultimately have on Ellie, who could grow up seeing her fathers being treated like this.

If you were the key worker, how would you respond?

The response

Written by a small group of practitioners in response to Scenario 3.

We know this sort of thing can happen because there is prejudice around and people hold strong views about gay men parenting young children. Some parents, who would not tolerate racist or sexist attitudes and behaviour, can seemingly, without question, hold strong homophobic views and behave with extraordinary prejudice towards gay parents. We all felt that if we were Chris or his partner, we should be outraged, upset, fearful even. If we were the key person, we think this would be a tough thing to handle well. What would we do?

We think the first thing to do is to listen to Chris, get all the facts of what happened and be clear that this behaviour is not tolerated in the setting (apart from being a matter of social justice, it's against the Equality Act 2012, so we would have to deal with it from a legal point of view). Chris needs to be supported, and he also needs information about his rights in the setting. There may well be formal processes of complaint as well as individual support for the family. Someone would need to talk with the father who was overheard hurling the abuse and make clear to him the policies of the setting, that homophobic bullying is unacceptable. Although undoing prejudice is a difficult thing and it takes time and a huge effort, day after day, we think that this is a bigger thing than James and Chris and Ellie. Unfortunately, this is about more than a lack of tolerance; it is outright discrimination. Does the setting have clear policies of inclusion that include gay and lesbian parents? How does a setting balance needs and rights and feelings of one family with another? How can families be supported in working towards a respect of difference and work on a basis that all are valued and have a contribution to make? We would use the materials and guidance available from Stonewall 'Education for All'[1] to work through this (Stonewall, 2010). This needs a lot of talking through and clear action.

In a survey of the experience of children and young people living with gay parents, Guasp (2011) reported that:

> ... Very young children don't think their families are different from other people's families at all.

> ... Children with gay parents like having gay parents and wouldn't want things to change but wish other people were more accepting.

> ... teachers think the word 'gay' is a bit like a swear word and they don't respond to anti-gay language in the same way they respond to racist language. (p. 3)

Workshop 5 Thinking inclusion

The four scenarios in this chapter are based on real situations. The role-plays which practitioners developed in response to them put them in a position of working out solutions by *thinking inclusively*.

These role-play experiences provided important data on the perspectives of practitioners on inclusive responses and challenges. Staff teams may wish to develop their own role-plays in response to the scenarios which form the basis of this chapter or they may prefer to develop some of their own from which to work out a role-play. The purpose of the exercise, which is freed to some extent from the constraints of specific workplace situations, is to work together by thinking inclusively to find solutions to scenarios which might otherwise lead to exclusive tendencies.

---

[1]Stonewall is a professional lobbying group promoting equality for lesbians, gay men and bisexuals. Stonewall's 'Education for All' campaign helps tackle homophobia and homophobic bullying in schools (see www.stonewall.org.uk/at_school/education_for_all/default.asp).

Policy points

Inclusion

In England
Policy suggests that inclusion is about ...

... 'a secure foundation through learning and development opportunities which are planned around the needs and interests of each individual child and are assessed and reviewed regularly.' (DfE, 2012, p. 12)

... 'celebrating uniqueness, nurturing positive, responsive relationships, providing environments which enable all children to learn and develop to their full potential.' (DfE, 2012, p. 3)

... 'relationships ... practitioners should link with, and help families to access, relevant services from other agencies as appropriate.' (DfE, 2012, p. 6)

In Scotland
'When supporting babies and young children through transitions, staff should ensure that they know them well enough to understand their needs and wishes.' (Learning and Teaching Scotland, 2010, p. 40)

The presence of an inclusive ethos is implied where staff plan and support play by:

- Knowing the importance of, and reflecting, cultural diversity, equality and inclusion in the planning and provision of play;
- Ensuring the development of positive relationships as part of the play experience;
- Knowing how to extend and support play in thoughtful and imaginative ways. (Learning and Teaching Scotland, 2010, pp. 75–6)

Children and young people are entitled to personal support to enable them to:

- 'Review their learning and plan for next steps';
- 'Gain access to learning activities which will meet their needs';

- 'Plan for opportunities for personal achievement';
- 'Prepare for changes and choices and be supported through changes and choices'. (Scottish Government, 2008, p. 21)

'The curriculum is the totality of experiences which are planned for children and young people through their education, wherever they are being educated. It includes the ethos and life of the school as a community; curriculum areas and subjects; interdisciplinary learning; and opportunities for personal achievement.' (Scottish Government, 2008, p. 23)

In Northern Ireland

'Well-planned, regular and skillful observations help teachers gain a more accurate picture of the progress each child is making across the whole curriculum. This in turn allows the teacher to plan a more relevant programme which will ensure that all children's needs are being met.' (CCEA, 2006, p. 14)

And

'For pupils with special educational needs teaching should take account of the type and extent of the difficulty experienced by the pupil. For pupils whose attainments fall significantly below the levels expected at a particular key stage, degrees of differentiation of tasks and materials appropriate to the age and requirements of the pupil will be necessary. For pupils whose attainments significantly exceed the expected levels of attainment during a particular key stage, teachers will need to plan suitably challenging work by extending the breadth and depth of study across Areas of Learning.' (CCEA, 2007, p. 3)

In Wales

The Framework for Children's Learning for 3–7 year-olds in Wales describes particular outcomes for young children. The significant adults in a child's life are called to accept responsibility to enable young children to achieve these outcomes. By embracing this accountability, young children can be supported to realise their potential ...

'Children have learned that they can and often do control their emotions. They have begun to form friendships which are very important to them, and idol/hero figures are significant in their play and lives. They understand that people have different preferences, views and beliefs and have an understanding of how they should relate to others morally and ethically. Children have moved on to be able to see things from other children's and adults' points of view. Children are competent in identifying problems and coming up with solutions to solve them. They are able to demonstrate skills of perseverance, concentration and motivation. They demonstrate appropriate self-control. Children understand how they can improve their learning and can be reflective.' (Welsh Assembly Government, 2008, p. 45)

Further reading

Connolly, P., Smith, A. and Kelly, B. (2002) *Too Young to Notice? The Cultural and Political Awareness of 3–6 Year Olds in Northern Ireland*. Belfast: Northern Ireland Community Relations Council.

Harris, N., Eden, K. with Blair, A. (2003) *Challenges to School Exclusion: Exclusion, Appeals and the Law*. London: Routledge Falmer.

Talking inclusion

Introduction

In this chapter, practitioners from the UK, Italy, Denmark and Greece discuss five key aspects of inclusion and we use these data to argue that greater cross-system understanding is needed: of curriculum, pedagogy and educational ethos.

The inclusion of young children in 'mainstream' generic settings is a matter for all practitioners. As we have seen throughout the book, UK policy developments, particularly in the area of the preschool curriculum, are broadly inclusive and our review of recent research into preschool educators' perspectives on special educational needs and inclusion has identified recurring themes and common concerns. This chapter uses illustrative extracts from questionnaires, email dialogues and face-to-face interviews taken from two studies – Study 1 (Nutbrown and Clough, 2004) and Study 2 (Clough and Nutbrown, 2004) – to discuss important themes identified by the practitioners who participated in our research. In particular, we stress the importance of developing understanding of curriculum, pedagogy and educational ethos across different types of early years settings.

Five key themes emerged from our research into practitioners' views of inclusion, about which all participants reported interesting views and concerns. These were:

- educators' personal experiences;
- professional development;
- views of childhood;
- inclusion and exclusion;
- the roles of parents.

In this chapter we use the words of participants from the two studies to discuss these themes. The important point in this chapter is that in order to fully understand each other and their practices, practitioners should 'talk inclusion'.

Study 1

Study 1 (Nutbrown and Clough, 2004) sought to broaden understanding of perspectives on teaching young children (0–7) with learning difficulties in a number of European countries and in a variety of educational approaches. This comparative study aimed to contribute to the development of policy through the articulation of a variety of effective practices that enhance living and learning experiences of young children who are disabled or who experience learning difficulties. This study took the form of a survey of preschool educators, working in a variety of forms of preschool education, in four European countries, and is organised around four key themes:

1 Practitioners' personal/professional experiences;
2 Professional development;
3 Inclusion and exclusion;
4 The roles of parents.

In all, 113 preschool educators from four European countries (Denmark, Greece, Italy and the UK) participated in the study. Data included 81 questionnaire responses, 21 email dialogues and 11 face-to-face interviews (see Table 6.1).

Table 6.1 Sources of data for Study 1

Country	Questionnaires	Email dialogues	Face-to-face interviews	Total respondents
Greece	19	4	5	28
UK	31	4	6	41
Denmark	12	6	0	18
Italy	19	7	0	26
Total	81 [72%]	21 [18%]	11 [10%]	113

Our aim was to take some 'snapshots' of views and practices from opportunistically available sources and thus we make no claims as to the representative nature of the sample. A range of settings and approaches were included in our sample, including educators working in fee-paying, charitable and state provision, and a range of curricular and pedagogic approaches. Table 6.2 shows the distribution of respondents across three types of preschool provision in the four countries.

Table 6.2   Distribution of respondents across three types of preschool provision in the four countries (Study 1)

Country	Total respondents	Independent fee-paying	Charitable/ voluntary	State/state funded
Greece	28	17	0	11
UK	41	11	11	19
Denmark	18	8	0	10
Italy	26	7	0	19
Total	*113*	*43 [38%]*	*11 [10%]*	*59 [52%]*

Postal and email questionnaires were distributed. Some participants chose to return anonymous responses while others added contact details and requested continued involvement in the project. Email dialogues emerged from exchanges (over about a three-week period) which began with the posing of pre-prepared questions and, as exchanges developed, included follow-up questions in response to participants' comments. The 11 face-to-face interviews each lasted between 65 and 100 minutes and were largely life-historical in nature. Computer-assisted analysis (using NVivo) of the three data sets led to the identification of four commonly shared themes.

Study 2

In Study 2, a parallel study of UK practitioners (Clough and Nutbrown, 2004), data were obtained from a total of 94 preschool educators from England, Northern Ireland, Scotland and Wales. Table 6.3 shows that respondents provided 68 questionnaire responses, 22 email dialogues and four face-to-face interviews. These (together with data from participants in Study 1 (Nutbrown and Clough, 2004)) form the basis of some of the findings reported in this chapter.

Table 6.3   Sources of data for Study 2

Country	Questionnaires	Email dialogues	Face-to-face interviews	Total respondents
England	18	4	2	24
Northern Ireland	14	6	0	20
Scotland	20	4	2	26
Wales	16	8	0	24
Total	*68*	*22*	*4*	*94*

Participants were volunteers who were contacted through a range of professional networks and development programmes. Thirty potential participants were contacted in each of the four countries of the UK, making a maximum potential response of 120. We suggest that the return of some 94 responses indicates the high interest and concern of professionals for the issues addressed in the study. The participants in the study were volunteers, and so we cannot claim them to be a representative sample of practitioners in the UK. However, their talk about inclusive issues has allowed us to take some snapshots of views and practices and to ensure a wide range of setting types and services are included. Questionnaires were administered both by post and email, and, as with Study 1, participants chose whether to add their contact details or to return anonymous responses. Email dialogues in Study 2 comprised a series of extended email exchanges (again, over a period of about three weeks) which included some pre-prepared questions and also follow-up discussions in response to participants' contributions. Life-historical, face-to-face interviews lasted around 90 minutes.

Interview and questionnaire schedules and email dialogue protocols were based on those developed in an earlier study (Nutbrown and Clough, 2003). All three methods of data collection addressed similar questions: career history; experiences of working with children with learning difficulties; professional development; opinions on inclusion; views on parental roles; and involvement. Questionnaires were brief, with ten questions in total. The face-to-face interviews and the extended email dialogues addressed the same themes as the question-naires but these two methods enabled us to probe more deeply into the responses given by research participants and so, in some cases, build a richer picture of respondents' thinking, values, beliefs and practices.

Table 6.4 shows the distribution of respondents in Study 2 across three types of preschool provision in England, Northern Ireland, Scotland and Wales.

Table 6.4 Distribution of respondents across three types of preschool provision in the four countries (Study 2)

Country	Total	LEA/ Foundation Stage	Independent fee-paying	Steiner-Waldorf	Montessori	Preschool/ playgroup
England	24	8	6	2	4	4
Northern Ireland	20	8	2	0	0	10
Scotland	26	6	6	2	0	12
Wales	24	10	4	0	0	10
Total	94	32	18	4	4	36

Educators' personal experiences

Across these settings and services respondents had a wide range of roles, responsibilities and backgrounds, and the sample included preschool educators working within a variety of curricular and pedagogic approaches. These included: local authority Foundation Stage nursery and reception classes; independent fee-paying nurseries; Steiner-Waldorf kindergartens; Montessori nursery schools and voluntary-run community preschool playgroups.

All but three respondents said they had some experience of working with children with learning difficulties – most with just one or two children, others having worked with many children with a variety of learning and developmental needs. The learning needs and difficulties most commonly listed as exceptionally demanding were:

- EBD (including ADHD);
- autistic spectrum disorder;
- multiple and physical learning difficulties.

Three respondents said they had specific responsibility for children with learning difficulties and all respondents, though their specific roles and responsibilities varied, shared the common experience of daily contact with young children in their work setting. The majority of participants in the study were working in provision that could be called 'generic' if not 'mainstream'. For example, Steiner-Waldorf Kindergartens and Montessori nursery schools would not be considered 'mainstream' but their provision for all children could be regarded as 'generic' rather than 'special' – as applied to the term special educational needs – in their overall disposition to the education of children with learning difficulties alongside their chronological peers.

We were told a number of stories about the development of professional careers during the life-historical interviews and email dialogues. A preschool playgroup leader from England told us:

> My sister was deaf, she went to a Deaf School and was residential from around about seven. I was nine then, and I . . . well, I 'lost' my sister. She learned, yes, no questions about that, but she lost so much – her family relationships, confidence with neighbours, she's still timid when she shops and meets strangers. When I started working with children – after I had my own – I decided that I would move heaven and earth to keep children with problems like hers in their own local schools. I'll take any child in the playgroup and fight tooth and nail for whatever they need to help them stay with us and go to the school next door.

Such career decisions are not always so directly related to key personal life events but accounts such as this are not uncommon and parents' experiences can offer a powerful voice in support of the inclusive project (Perera, 2001). Clough has suggested that individual practitioners' routes to inclusive education are seldom 'accidental' and that there may well be, for some, a purposeful (if sometimes unconscious) seeking out of work in SEN and inclusive settings (Clough and Corbett, 2000).

Professional development

Professional development opportunities for preschool educators was an issue which generated much comment and surprisingly few felt appropriately equipped for working with children with learning difficulties. Table 6.5 shows that the majority of practitioners who participated in the study reported that the main part of their understanding and knowledge was derived 'on the job' through experience in teaching young children with learning difficulties as and when such children joined their settings.

Table 6.5   Rating of professional development and the impact of experience on educators' professional insight and knowledge

Country	Total	High Level	Adequate	Poor	Derived from experience
England	24	4	14	6	22
Northern Ireland	20	2	14	4	20
Scotland	26	3	19	4	22
Wales	24	1	19	3	25
Total	*94*	*11*	*66*	*17*	*89*

Typical comments were:

> *I've spoken with the speech therapist and occupational therapist when they have visited about individual children.* (Nursery nurse in Northern Ireland)

> *I've spoken with children's social workers and health visitors and the early years adviser.* (Playgroup co-ordinator in Northern Ireland)

> *I've had no professional development really. Occasional training but not always when required.* (Preschool leader in Aberdeenshire)

> *I've had Autism Awareness training, however, I don't feel qualified or really informed enough to give the support children with SEN deserve.* (Nursery teacher in Wales)

A few respondents felt their professional development was of a high level, such as:

> *I've had a lot of training over my career. Specific things like developing children's language skills, supporting children in the Autistic Spectrum, and general stuff on*

the Code of Practice, Target Setting and Action Planning. (Early Years Centre manager in England)

I've had training through the local education authority and the EYDCP as a SEN Co-ordinator and opportunities to work with experts in Special needs. I've also followed Steiner Curative Therapy training. All of these experiences are useful. (Steiner-Waldorf kindergarten teacher in England)

I did an M.Ed and specialised in SEN and young children. Fantastic, I learned so much and became my own 'expert'. I still read so much, particularly around managing behaviour and particular EBD issues. (Nursery teacher in Scotland)

Most early years practitioners in the study who reported that they valued their professional development in the field highly were experienced professionals who had studied at postgraduate level, having been awarded diplomas or Masters degrees in areas related to early education, special educational needs and inclusion.

Views of childhood

Some interesting concepts about childhood emerged in the data. Respondents' views of early childhood were categorised into two broad areas. The first area comprised childhood as a vulnerable state where adults must protect and shield children from risk. Examples of this view included comments such as:

All young children need to be nurtured. Childhood is such a vulnerable time, whatever children's needs, we must protect them from threats to their bodies and souls. (Steiner kindergarten teacher in England)

Little children are so at risk, aren't they? It's such a responsibility to try to protect them from all sorts of horrors. We have to try to do that for all of them in the early years, Special Needs or not. (Teacher in Northern Ireland)

This is an important time of calm and quiet discovery. The environment should be such that children can learn without distraction or worry. (Montessori teacher in England)

The second area comprised childhood as a time of discovery, of oneself as well as of knowledge of the world, where adults have the responsibility to support and encourage. Typical comments in this category were:

I think it's part of my job to get each one of them to have a go – be bold! So I push them a bit to try things – even if they struggle and they might have SEN or something – but I want them to take a risk, they don't need mollycoddling! (Nursery teacher in Wales)

I think disabled children should be given opportunities like the rest, let them try things, it's no good keeping them confined in case they have trouble. (Day nursery leader in Scotland)

Inclusion and exclusion

When we asked the preschool educators in our survey whether children should be included, a small few were unequivocal advocates for full inclusion:

> Absolutely, there's too much segregation in society. Young children should learn about differences and – before prejudices are formed – they can experience living together with others who are different. (Teacher in Northern Ireland)

Table 6.6 shows the three categories of response from the participants who said they believed either that all children be included or that children should be included 'in principle' or that children with learning difficulties should not be included. Of the few who were unequivocal about the importance of inclusion for all, one said:

> Yes, I feel the only way forward is through integration. (Nursery nurse in Northern Ireland)

Table 6.6 Educators' beliefs on inclusion and exclusion (Study 2)

Country	Total	All children should be included	Inclusion in principle, but depends on difficulties	No inclusion for children with Learning Difficulties
England	24	3	19	2
Northern Ireland	20	9	8	3
Scotland	26	8	16	2
Wales	24	4	17	3
Total	94	24	60	10

As with Study 1 involving European educators (Nutbrown and Clough, 2004), the most commonly-held view was positively for inclusion in principle, but many respondents set out conditions around support, resources and the effect of other pupils. We have referred to such a view as the 'yes – but...' factor. Thus, some practitioners said:

> Yes – but depending on the nature of their individual challenge and the ability of the teacher to support effectively that special need in her setting. (Steiner-Waldorf kindergarten teacher in England)

> Yes, when children with SEN are in mainstream classes it promotes their overall development, however, consideration to the adult/child ratio should be given. For example, the classroom assistant may be needed so as not to hinder other children's progression. (Playgroup assistant in Northern Ireland)

Yes, in some cases, but not all. It must be beneficial to the SEN child but not disruptive to the other children. (Nursery nurse in Wales)

Not necessarily, however it is often good for both sides to support and be supported by each other. It is wonderful to see how accepting and naturally supportive non-SEN children can be – they also learn patience, tolerance and generosity. (Steiner teacher in England)

Six respondents said that children with learning difficulties should not be included, arguing:

No, some children cannot tolerate the presence of their peers and become very distressed. (Playleader in Scotland)

No, because they'd be better off in a specialist centre. (Assistant teacher and SENCO in Montessori school England)

Many of our 'yes – but....' respondents identified the availability of adequate support for the child and staff as the key issue which makes for successful inclusion. Resources for such support have been earlier identified as crucial (Croll and Moses, 2000), although it is often as much a matter of professional willingness and responsiveness as of effective use of additional support resources (Karsten et al., 2001). Emanuelsson (2001) suggests that it is *teaching* rather than children that needs support. Whether the need for support is perceived by practitioners simply because they feel that if a child has a specific difficulty there must inevitably be a need for additional support in order effectively to include pupils with learning difficulties or whether support needs are identified as part of a realistic review of a child's needs, participants in the study confirmed that issues of support are often a major concern when inclusion is under consideration, and some talked of being fearful of a lack of support if and when it was needed.

The roles of parents

As might be expected in a survey of early childhood educators, there was broad agreement that, in the early years, parents should be involved in their children's learning and development programmes (see Table 6.7). Examination of their comments uncovered differing views of what such involvement meant.

As much involvement as possible, as this gives parents a greater understanding of what is being achieved and then parents can reinforce these values in the home. (Montessori teacher in England)

There should be close links with the group and the home. Activities which we can use on the advice of the educational psychologist can help parents continue work at home. (Nursery nurse in Scotland)

As much involvement as possible, they know their children better than a specialist.
(Day nursery manager in Scotland)

Table 6.7 Educators' beliefs on parental involvement

Country	Total	Full parental involvement	Some parental involvement but...	No parental involvement
England	24	20	3	1
Northern Ireland	20	17	1	2
Scotland	26	20	6	0
Wales	24	14	6	4
Total	94	71	16	7

Some behavioural difficulties have been explained by a lack of parental support for children at home:

> *Some parents struggle too, with their own literacy and lifestyles. That creates difficulties for their children.* (Preschool playgroup worker in Wales)

Arguments for the non-involvement of parents, giving them information but not consulting them as partners, were based on views that parents themselves struggled with many problems. A small number of participants felt that their involvement in preschool would exacerbate existing difficulties for the children and staff. In all cases where such comments were made, the children cited were identified as having EBD. One teacher said:

> *Sometimes it's just so painful for parents to hear the awful things their children do, and what professionals say about them. I just wonder if it's better for them not to be so involved in all the meetings and things. I feel sorry for them, especially when they've got other difficulties themselves.* (Nursery teacher in England)

And another:

> *Oh! Sometimes they just make it worse. I know that's a horrid thing to say, but if I could just get on with it sometimes, but some parents make me feel it's my fault their children behave so badly! I suppose they don't mean to, and, well, one particular mother, she, well, she just has to get at somebody – so it seems that it's me. Wears you out though...* (Nursery teacher in Wales)

These views were not common, and the following expressions were much more typical of the overall view in our sample:

> *Parents are their children's primary educators. I really believe that – they're not with us that long. Of course parents must be involved.* (Playgroup worker in Northern Ireland)

Overwhelmingly, it was suggested that parents should be included because:

- parents need information about processes, systems and intervention strategies;
- parents have ultimate responsibility for the care and education of their children;
- fundamentally, parents spend more time with and have the most intimate knowledge of their children.

The literature on parental involvement in preschool education in general supports the latter view and as such the view of participants in our survey comes as no surprise.

Conclusion

In this chapter we have shown how practitioners can, individually and collectively, discuss their thoughts on inclusion and inclusive practices. What they have said here sets the scene for the next three chapters which focus on practical development in including children, parents and practitioners in the learning communities of which they are a part.

Workshop 6 Talking inclusion

In our study, practitioners made the following statements about inclusion. Staff groups could use a selection of these to begin their discussion on their own views on inclusive practices and as starting points to talking inclusion.

... there's too much segregation in society. Young children should learn about differences and – before prejudices are formed – they can experience living together with others who are different.

Yes – but depending on the nature of their individual challenge and the ability of the teacher to support effectively that special need in her setting.

... when children with SEN are in mainstream classes it promotes their overall development, however, consideration to the adult/child ratio should be given. For example, the classroom assistant may be needed so as not to hinder other children's progression.

... in some cases, but not all. It must be beneficial to the SEN child but not disruptive to the other children.

Not necessarily, however it is often good for both sides to support and be supported by each other. It is wonderful to see how accepting and naturally supportive non-SEN children can be – they also learn patience, tolerance and generosity.

No, some children cannot tolerate the presence of their peers and become very distressed.

No, because they'd be better off in a specialist centre.

Sometimes it's just so painful for parents to hear the awful things their children do, and what professionals say about them. I just wonder if it's better for them not to be so involved in all the meetings and things. I feel sorry for them, especially when they've got other difficulties themselves.

Policy points

Reflecting on the discussion in this chapter, we can see how policy is played out across the four countries of the UK.

In England
'Every child deserves the best possible start in life and the support that enables them to fulfil their potential.' (DfE, 2012, p. 2)

In Scotland
'All children have the right to a safe environment in which to learn, develop, play and thrive.' (Learning and Teaching Scotland, 2010, p. 58)

And

'Every child and young person should know they are valued and will be supported to become a successful learner, an effective contributor, a confident individual and a responsible citizen'. (Scottish Government, 2008, p. 11)

In Northern Ireland
'Without the use of regular observations and written records on each child's development, the teacher is left with an incomplete picture of the child. This may lead to the loss of significant information that could help shape planning and take more account of each child's needs.' (CCEA, 2006, p. 13)

'Throughout the primary stages teachers should help children to become aware of some of their rights and responsibilities.' (CCEA, 2007, p. 4)

In Wales
'We aim to ensure that all children and young people have a flying start in life and the best possible basis for their future growth and development.' (Welsh Assembly Government, 2008, p. 3)

Further reading 📖

Clough, P. and Nutbrown, C. (2004) Special educational needs and inclusive early education: multiple perspectives from UK educators. *Journal of Early Childhood Research*, 2(2): 191–211.

Nutbrown, C. and Clough, P. (2004) Inclusion in the early years: conversations with European educators. *European Journal of Special Needs Education*, 19(3): 311–39.

7

Including children

Introduction

> Respectful educators will include all children; not just children who are
> easy to work with, obliging, endearing, clean, pretty, articulate, capable,
> but every child – respecting them for who they are, respecting their lan-
> guage, their culture, their history, their family, their abilities, their
> needs, their name, their ways and their very essence. (Nutbrown, 1996,
> p. 54)

In this chapter we explore what it might mean for settings actively to
pursue the inclusion of all young children through a curriculum and
pedagogy which have at their centre the ethos of inclusion. Such settings
must examine their practices in terms of how the voices of *all* the
children in them are listened to and how each and every child attending
those settings can be said to be included as a respected citizen of their
early years communities.

Because, as we argued at the outset of the book, inclusive *policies* are, in
fact, only realised in acts of inclusive *practices*, much of this chapter is
built around a number of small-scale studies which have, in various ways,
developed and evaluated strategies for including children. The accounts
here show how complex and serious a matter it is self-consciously to create *truly* inclusive early years settings. Our intention in this chapter is
to demonstrate, through this collection of studies of including young
children, how settings must interrogate every single aspect of their practices for opportunities to create inclusive experiences for the children
they serve.

We begin, though, with a consideration of how young children are
viewed by practitioners, for it is not necessarily the case that all early
years practitioners would hold the same views about children or, indeed,

share similar 'constructions' of childhood. As part of our CAPE (Comparative Approaches to Preschool Education) study we asked practitioners to talk about their views (constructions) of childhood. First, we asked them to consider two common but polarised views of childhood:

- childhood as a vulnerable state where adults must protect and shield children from risk; and
- childhood as a time of discovery, of oneself as well as of knowledge of the world, where adults have the responsibility to support and encourage.

We asked them to talk about the following two statements:

All young children need to be nurtured, childhood is such a vulnerable time, whatever children's needs, we must protect them from threats to their bodies, and souls. (Steiner kindergarten teacher in England)

I think it's part of my job to get each one of them to have a go – be bold! So I push them a bit to try things – even if they struggle and they might have SEN or something – but I want them to take a risk, they don't need mollycoddling! (Nursery teacher in Wales)

Participants' responses fell, not surprisingly, into two broad groups which reflect the polarisations: first, those who saw children as vulnerable, and secondly, those who felt they were discoverers who needed challenge and risk to encourage their learning in the early years. The following discussion helps to illuminate the complexity of thinking behind these two, apparently opposite, positions:

Clare: I agree with the first one. I think… Well… I think they need love and looking after, and – well – protecting… yeah – protection from all the horrid stuff that goes on… I mean, well, yeah, they need to try things out but…

Siobhan: You have to let them free though… It's tough out there and you…

Clare: There's time enough to get tough later… I want them to have a sense of nurture and protection.

Mia: Isn't that for the parents, though?

Clare: Yes, but I think…

Mia: We need to help them widen their horizons…

Astrid: Yes – take risks…

Siobhan: It's a tough world – they need to develop a thick skin and…

Clare: Not when you're only four!

The conversation concluded with a general view that a balance needs to be struck. Yet there was an interesting blend of pedagogies and personal life histories here, which surely had some continuity with the various views held. Siobhan explained how her father had died when she was very young and how she quickly learned that there was no Father Christmas and food did not magically appear on the table – which is why she said 'they need a thick skin'. Clare, who felt that 'love and looking after and protection' were important, explained how she – an only child – had lived an 'idyllic' childhood in a tiny Scottish village with, as she said, 'No fear, no worries, and surrounded by loving interested adults'.

Constructions of childhoods and hence beliefs of what children 'need' and how they should be educated in the early years are inevitably influenced by the life experiences of the adults who work with them. As Boyden (1997) argues, childhood is (for some children) 'a very unhappy time' paralleled by 'adult nostalgia for youthful innocence'. The diverse range of views about childhood described by participants in this study demonstrates quite clearly that there is no 'one childhood' and that complex social constructions of 'childhood' (Anderson, 1980) inform practitioners' beliefs *about* childhood and their practices *with* children.

It is important for practitioners clearly to articulate their personal constructions of childhood and to understand how such deeply personal views about childhood can influence their responses to, expectations of, and work with, young children.

One of the things which became clear in all the examples which make up this chapter, are the implicit underpinning beliefs which practitioners hold about the children for whom they are responsible. And it is this crucial underpinning which, we suggest, enables practitioners to tackle the difficult, subtle and complex issues in order to create inclusive early years communities. In the remainder of this chapter, various practitioners report aspects of their research into areas of practice which contribute to inclusive pedagogy. We begin with a discussion of how babies might be included in their settings and conclude with work on supporting children to include their playground peers.

Including babies and toddlers

Including babies means finding ways to listen to them and becoming sensitised to their needs and wants. Such listening is no easy skill to develop for it requires the development of a deep and intimate knowing of each baby – and their ways are different and forms of communication unique. Listening to babies and responding to their interests and impulses requires an attentiveness which is quite different from that needed for work with children who are even only a year older. Let us try to explain what we mean when we say that including babies must begin with listening to them.

A child minder took 13 month old Demetrius to watch the trains. She held his hands and patiently supported him as he walked up the steps of the footbridge and bent beside him – her arms around his tummy – as he looked through the railings on the top of the footbridge. In the distance a train was approaching. Demetrius loves the trains and this little outing to watch them go under the bridge was one of his favourite events of any day. As the train came nearer two strangers walked over the footbridge. Demetrius took his eyes off the train and his gaze fixed on the strangers as they approached him, smiled at him and continued past. Demetrius's childminder gently turned his head, reverting his eyes to the train which was about to pass under the bridge. Demetrius struggled slightly in an attempt to continue watching the new people he was so fascinated by, but his childminder had brought him to see the trains and, from her point of view, he was missing the event he usually so enjoyed. What is important here, we suggest, is that listening to babies and toddlers requires constant vigilance and perpetual checking of the adult agenda so that when children's interests change as subtly as they did for Demetrius, that adult can identify such shifts and further support new interests.

Such a task is not easy, partly because babies' and toddlers' agendas are constantly changing, but it is, we suggest, a crucial part of inclusive practices with babies and an important part of hearing the multiple voices of the youngest learners.

In a busy hotel restaurant, two babies were having breakfast with their families. They were each sitting in a high chair, having been offered a collection of yogurt, fruit and so on. The two babies were separated by three other tables and other diners and waiting staff were walking past during the morning bustle around the breakfast buffet. One of the babies spotted the other. After a while he received a smile of acknowledgement from the other. Over several minutes, unnoticed by their parents, the two babies shared an exchange – smiling, gesturing and, without doubt, enjoying the communication they had established. Before long the mothers noticed this subtle exchange and they also exchanged a smile of recognition, seemingly pleased that their babies had spotted each other. The interaction between the two continued with one of the fathers adjusting the angle of his son's high chair to make it easier for him to see and communicate with the other baby. The two families continued with the breakfast while the babies continued their exchange, unhurried and without adult interference. They were interrupted when another guest, who had met one family the day before, came up to the child and started to smile and talk to him. Although he tried to look around her and to avoid her attempts to engage him, she persisted, unaware of what she had interrupted. The point of this story is that adults, in their attempts to engage with young children, need to take care not to interrupt the pursuits that children have chosen for themselves. Here the baby boy's agenda (supported by his parents) was to communicate with another baby that he had found nearby; the woman's agenda, it seemed, was meeting her own need to engage with the baby, oblivious of his present interests. Well meant, though it was, her attempt to engage him interrupted his own 'conversation'.

There are times when adults are so intent on following their own agenda (often created in what they feel to be in the child's best interests) that things can go wrong in terms of respecting young children's rights and allowing them to participate in their own decisions.

Eighteen month-old Sarah was at the dentist for the first time. She was not happy. In the waiting room she repeatedly said to her father ''ome now – go 'ome now?' Her father explained that they were all going to see the dentist and he wanted to see her lovely little white teeth. Sarah clamped her mouth shut and stuck out her bottom lip (she appeared to be quite certain that no one was going to see her teeth that day!). The family went into the dentist surgery and before long Sarah appeared in her mother's arms – she was sobbing and saying 'No, no mister – no like that mister'. Sarah's mum tried everything.

> 'Show me – show me your teeth.'
> 'Show teddy.'
> 'Show this mirror.'
> Sarah opened her mouth wide and looked at her own teeth in the mirror. She seemed very happy now.
> 'Now – will you show that Mister your teeth?'
> 'No!' Sarah stamps her foot.
> 'Do you want all your teeth to fall out?'
> 'No!'
> 'Then show him your teeth. They'll all fall out.'
> 'No!' Sarah is in tears and stamping her foot.
> 'No! No mouth.'

There is nothing malicious or deliberately unkind here. Sarah's mother wants her teeth to stay healthy – she's trying to act in Sarah's interests. What goes wrong here is the lack of listening – really listening to Sarah's wishes and the urgency with which the dental check up is pursued. Perhaps more time, another visit, less rush might have helped Sarah feel much more part of the decision to visit the dentist and have her routine check-up?

Listening to babies is a crucial part of planning curricula for them and of developing pedagogies which allow them to follow their own specific and unique interests. The following observation of a baby – at home – exploring his own treasure basket shows how sensitive adults can support children's persistent interests and include them in making decisions about their own learning (see Box 7.1).

Box 7.1   Matthew's treasure basket

At 6 months old and able to sit up, Matthew was just the right age to begin his exploration of the natural materials offered to him in his Treasure Basket. At the time of the observation, Matthew, who had just turned 9 months old, was used to handling, mouthing, sorting and selecting his favourite items from his basket.

Matthew's mother, places the treasure basket with its abundance of natural materials in the middle of a large cleared space in the room. She then asks Matthew gently if he would like to play with his treasure. He waves his arms and legs frantically as his eyes rest on the basket. Kate places Matthew close enough for him to reach right into the basket. He immediately reaches in with his right hand and selects a long wooden handled spatula. 'Oohh, ahh', he says and looks directly at his mother. She smiles at him in approval. Still holding the spatula he proceeds to kneel up and lean across the basket in order to reach a long brown silk scarf. He pulls at the scarf and squeals in delight as he pulls the fabric through his fingers. 'Oohh, ahh', he repeats. He lets go of the spatula and abandons the scarf to his side. His eyes rest on a large blue stone, he picks up the large stone with his right hand and turns it over on his lap using both hands. Still using both hands he picks the stone up and begins to bite it, making a noise as his teeth grind against the hard surface. He smiles, looking at his mother as he repeatedly bites the stone over and over again. He stops, holds the stone up to his face and looks at it intently, then puts it to his mouth once more. He then picks up the wooden spatula again and while holding it firmly in one hand, he turns the contents of the basket over with his other hand, squealing loudly with delight as he discovers the matching long-handled fork. Matthew looks at his mother and waves both items in the air smiling and rocking on his knees saying 'Oohh, ahh'. He turns away from the basket and waves the long-handled implements up and down in his hands, first one then the other then both together. He turns back to the basket with a puzzled expression and for a few seconds stops waving the items. He drops the fork and reaches back into the basket and randomly picks up items one at a time, looks at them and then discards them on the floor beside him. He continues this pattern for several seconds until he comes upon a long-handled brush. He picks up the brush, pauses and then waves it in his left hand, all the time continuing to hold the wooden spatula in his right hand. For several seconds he proceeds to bang the long-handled items together, smiling as the two wooden items make a sound as they came together. He then spots the wooden fork he

(Continued)

(Continued)

had disposed of earlier and letting go of the brush picks up the wooden fork and bangs it together with the spatula. 'Baba, baba, da, da, da', he says, then a little more loudly he repeats 'baba, baba, da, da, da'. Just when it seems that he is giving signals that he has finished with the items in the basket he notices another long scarf. Letting go of both the wooden items he reaches into the basket and tugs the scarf. He pulls it over his face and blows raspberries. He smiles at his mother and she smiles at him. The material falls to the floor and Matthew looks up at his mother and waves his arms up and down. Kate, realising that Matthew is signalling that he has finished with his treasure basket for today, reaches down and holds her arms out to him. Matthew instantly smiles, holds his arms up to her. As she sweeps him into her arms, Matthew snuggles into his mother's neck and with his thumb in his mouth utters his contented 'kai, kai, kai' sound. (Nutbrown, 2010, p. 117)

Listening, as the above examples show, is an essential skill of any adult working with the youngest children who are, according to Powell, powerless and vulnerable:

> Very young children represent one of the least powerful groups in society and have no real way to resist any discrimination and prejudice that they may experience and which may have a devastating impact on their lives. (Powell, 2005, p. 79)

The *Birth to Three Matters* framework (DfES, 2002) provided practitioners with a tool to develop inclusive practice when working with babies and children under 3 years. The framework took an holistic approach to supporting young children's learning with inclusive practices firmly embedded in every element of the document. In order to ensure that practitioners can fully understand and work through the pack, it has been divided into four colour-coded aspects which are then further divided into 16 components. 'A Strong Child' is the aspect which emphasises the importance of a child's ability to realise their own identity. This theme is further developed and linked in the aspects 'A Skilful Communicator', 'A Competent Learner' and 'A Healthy Child'. Though no longer government policy in England, the framework is available as a resource for practitioners at (4children – www.4children. org.uk.)

It is good practice for children to develop close relationships with a 'key person' who provides continuity of care for the child and lessens the separation anxiety for the child/parent relationship (Goldschmied and Jackson, 1994; Penn, 1999). The same practitioner works with the same baby each day, feeding, changing nappies and interacting with the baby in a close, respectful and dignified manner. By observing children closely, the adult can ensure that the views of the child are respected and upheld, irrespective of the age of the child. Where a baby is to be looked after in an out-of-home setting, the importance of a 'key person' cannot be over emphasised and requires careful planning to ensure that *all* the needs of the child and the family can be met by the practitioners who will care for the child, particularly where there may be additional factors to consider. It is this ethos that is fundamental to the key person approach and what makes it unique. As Elfer, Goldschmied and Selleck (2003, p. 43) propose: 'Failure to take account of these underlying anxieties explains why some nurseries' key person approaches do not seem to translate into practice'.

'Listening to Young Children', a resource developed by Coram Family to support parents and practitioners, gives examples of how to 'include' the very youngest children, to help practitioners and parents listen and to ensure the children have a voice and that adults can respond accordingly and appropriately (Lancaster, 2003). Babies deserve to be given the opportunity to grow and develop in the security of a community that affords them respect, with practitioners who see the world through the child's eyes. It is easier perhaps to comprehend listening and responding to the views of 3 and 4 year olds who are able to articulate their desires and dislikes, but inclusion requires that all children should express needs and wants and not be 'done unto' without consultation or consideration. This applies to the very youngest children, to babies, offering opportunities for their voices to be heard and expressed not just in speech but through play, actions, facial expressions and so on (Pugh and Selleck, 1996).

Including young children

Among the many challenges that the development of inclusive practices offers us are the ways in which children might participate – or at least 'have a say' – in the things that matter to them. Lancaster (2003) states that:

> A newborn baby is beginning to tell stories by looking into the eyes of others, posing silent questions, asking for co-operation for understanding a common world. (p.7)

Including young children is no easy matter. Being actively thorough about developing and maintaining inclusive practices means staying alert to all that happens and being prepared to engage in personal interrogation of everything that happens. Perhaps one of the most personally challenging acts of inclusion is the overt involvement of young children in their own emotional and moral development. Dyer's work (see Box 7.2) is an example of how the challenge to create an emotionally literate nursery can be developed.

Box 7.2   Developing emotional intelligence in a nursery community

Dyer (2002) carried out an ethnographic study to explore ways of developing emotional intelligence in a nursery class. Using the *Box Full of Feelings* (Moons and Kog, 1997), Dyer focused specifically on helping children to recognise certain emotions – anger, sadness, happiness, fear – in themselves and others and, by developing ideas already in use in the nursery, she and her team sought to increase children's sense of emotional well-being. The study focused on four main areas: the need for emotionally intelligent adults; the importance of friendship and play; storytelling and emotional intelligence; children's moral awareness. Dyer writes:

> The purpose of this research was not so much to mould useful future citizens as to empower individuals. The project focused on the children, but it quickly became evident that it should also include the emotional and ethical quality of relationships between children and staff, staff and parents and among the staff. The research focus also made it easier to discuss curriculum values, aims and innovations, as we became clearer about ethical and emotional implications. As an example, Gussin Paley, in *You can't say 'you can't play'* (1992), argues that it is unfair and morally untenable to expect children to deal unaided with social rejection and its consequences; that adults have a responsibility to change the order of things, however long it has been accepted as natural. It took much careful preparation and many illustrative and exploratory stories, but when we officially established the rule *'You can't say you can't play'* the children were not only supported but also relieved … (2002, p. 69)

Children and adults need to learn together about emotional intelligence. Children are not passive recipients – they have much to teach adults – and their attitudes to each other continually challenge adults to reassess their own views. Matthews (1994) and Nutbrown (1996) both write about how taking the perspectives of children into serious account might radically alter our accepted values and codes of behaviour.

Sophie's treatment of the other children was something we all wrestled with … the necessity for dialogue – children with children, and children with adults – as we work through things together, not always getting it right, but needing to trust people's good intentions. …

Kizzie observed that Sophie was angry (biting people) 'cos they wouldn't be her friend, so be her friend and she won't hit you. She doesn't hit me. Later (a month later) Sophie bit her hard. Too much, Kizzie distressed, rejecting Sophie (as Sophie had her in a way). My solution later (after Sophie had resumed hitting) was to address the whole group again – we all love her but this hitting has to stop. All started saying what she'd done to them, I dismayed, not what I'd intended. Sophie didn't want to listen. Her mum said Sophie wouldn't hit unless other children were being mean to her, and Sophie had been worried to come to school, was scared.

We have to let this play out, don't we? Sophie needs that reaction, absolute moral rules – you *break* faith, people *lose* faith. But Coles (1997, p. 195) reiterates what I understood before, simply 'be kind', rather than thinking in terms of what's the best thing to do. Coles says he pushed for answers, as a 'worried, literal-minded father, teacher'. But what he got was 'I told you … you have to be kind, that's what we have to be, to *do*: show by how we behave that we're interested in others and want the best for them.' And isn't that what Kizzie wanted for Sophie? Isn't it a question of our keeping faith with Sophie?

Sophie pinched May and Bella because 'dey darfed at me when I dell over.' I was saying it was worse to pinch, but is it (colleague W) asked? She's right.

Sophie knocked down Susie and Destiny's brick house. Both cross with her. Destiny came to me to complain. We talked to Sophie – 'are people allowed to knock down other's models?' Uncomfortable. She came to say sorry and kissed Susie. Susie won over, pretended to fall over with goofy look, Sophie delighted, Susie kissed *her*. Sophie now the centre, both Destiny and Susie saying – 'you *can* come in our house, you can come in our car'. Very friendly, inviting, welcoming. Sophie entranced.

Sophie walking round nursery all morning with Tom bear in her arms, tender, solicitous, making sure he has the right clothes, asking me to help her put them on, full of love for Tom. Every now and then came to say, with conscious expression, as she bit him or hit him on the head, 'I diting Tom bear/I durting 'im'. And I would say, 'but he knows you love him?' and she'd smile and hug him tightly.

Sophie stood up on the mermaid chair (a place to make announcements) red splodge painting held up – and announced 'It's Happy!' (What a testimonial!) Everyone clapped.

Inclusive practices can be developed in ways which recognise that children themselves can be important agents for inclusion. Carter's work on Playground Buddies (Carter, 2005; summarised in Box 7.3) illustrates how young children can be supported by adults in order to enable them, in turn, to support their lonelier peers in the playground.

Box 7.3   The playground buddies

The aim of the Playground Buddies project was to examine children's perspectives on the experience of being a Playground Buddy and to find out how effective training and support for the buddies proved to be for the children.

The school where the study took place was a small, mixed community for children aged 4–7 years. In an affluent working-class area, the percentage of children on free school meals was below the national average, many families had their own small businesses and some were in professional careers. The intake is one of predominantly white British and English speaking. Few children speak English as an additional language and the number identified as having special educational needs is below the national average.

Learning through play is a strong part of the ethos of the school and considerable work had already been done on playing outdoors and on behaviour and relationships. A clear aim was to ensure that children had a positive playtime experience and were able to re-enter the classroom ready to engage and focus on learning.

Playground Buddies are a group of children who have applied to do the job during playtimes. They need to be willing to help their peers, play games, help lonely children to make friends, bring out and put away equipment or sit with an unwell child to keep them company (Mosley 2001). Playtimes at the school ran relatively smoothly. However, the school wanted to be proactive in supporting unhappy or lonely children, children frightened of being bullied, children without friends and so on. The Playground Buddy project was very much part of extending Personal Social and Emotional Development and the Citizenship Curriculum.

Details of research questions, methodology and ethical considerations are reported elsewhere (Carter, 2005), but key findings from the study focused around four main themes: loneliness; playground friends support network; challenges; status and social skills.

Loneliness

Most children reported that they would feel sad and lonely if they had no one to play with. Bob gave a real insight into his own experience before becoming a playground friend.

Bob:	It made me feel sad when I was lonely when I wasn't a playground friend.
R (Researcher):	So when you weren't a playground friend you were lonely?
Bob:	Yes.
R:	Was that because you had nobody to play with?
Bob:	I had no one to play with. I was always at the Friendship Stop and no one saw me.
R:	OK, could you get help from anyone or did you have to stay lonely?
Bob:	No.
R:	Did you ever mention it to an adult?
Bob:	No.

R: No, you just stayed lonely.
Bob: Yes.
R: How did you feel?
Bob: I just felt bored and annoyed
R: Who did you feel annoyed with?
Bob: I felt annoyed by having no one to play with.
R: And you couldn't tell anybody?
Bob: No.
R: Poor you, I'm glad things have been better for you. It's really good now they're better. When you stop being a playground friend, if you found yourself lonely again, what do you think you could do?
Bob: I could tell a teacher.
R: What else could you do?
Bob: Ask a playground friend.

Bob's response did indicate that for him, the Playground Buddies experience had been a success. He had had lots of children to play with and for him this has been the thing he liked most about being a playground friend.

The support network

Most children talked about where they could get help if they needed it. Figure 7.1 is taken from one of the Playground Buddies' journals. Beneath it the teacher has written the child's words: 'These are the other playground friends. They help people too.' This picture was drawn by a child who had received training in how to be a playground buddy and shows the playground friends wearing the distinctive hats which helped children to identify them. Drawing all the playground friends together suggests the strength of the support network and bond that had developed. Playground friends went to each other for support in helping their peers.

Figure 7.1 Playground buddies

(Continued)

(Continued)

The challenges of being a Playground Buddy

During training for their role, children identified two main problems: the volume of children at the 'Friendship Stop' and how to help them all; how to support the youngest children in the school. Ideas for changes and improvements were discussed with the children and resulted in possible strategies, such as the one in Figure 7.2 which reads: 'When a lot of people is at the Friendship Stop think up a game for them'. This idea was included among others in a training manual that was produced for future Playground Buddies.

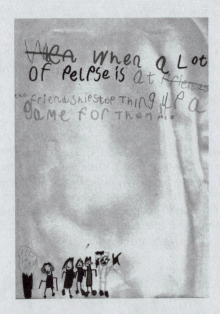

Figure 7.2 'When a lot of people is at the Friendship Stop think up a game for them!!'

Status and social skills gained from being a Playground Buddy

The children's journals included many examples which demonstrated that children who were Playground Buddies gained something in terms of status and social skills. The most fascinating examples were those that indicated that children felt a sense of pride and raised self-esteem from having helped others. Figures 7.3a and 7.3b show two journal extracts. They consist of lists that children started to compile of the children that they helped while they were Playground Buddies. Keeping records clearly mattered to the children, thus indicating the degree of importance which they attached to the role.

Figures 7.3a   Journal entries (1).

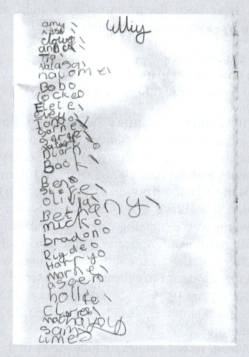

Figures 7.3b   Journal entries (2).

(Continued)

(Continued)

The Playground Buddies project highlighted several issues:

- There were children experiencing loneliness and having few or no friends (Dunn, 2004). The Playground Buddy could help here.
- Children who were Playground Buddies felt comfortable or drawn to helping younger children (Furman et al., 1979).
- Making changes to the Playground Buddy system following discussions with the children led to insights and improvements.
- Children need to be prepared for and equipped with skills to be a Playground Buddy (Mosely 2001).
- Playground Buddies can support more vulnerable children (Shotton, 1998).

The Playground Buddies in this study benefited from training and ongoing adult support, which incorporated a 'pedagogy of listening' (Rinaldi, 1999).

Children's views of their early years settings

It is only in the last decade or so, that the children, the 'users' of preschool groups, have been deemed to have a right and an ability to express their views. Some researchers are now:

- researching children's views;
- focusing on child 'participation';
- attending to 'voice' – the otherwise 'silent' or less powerful.

Until recently, it was unusual for the views of children and young people of any age, let alone very young children, to be consulted on aspects of their experience in educational settings (Kirby and Bryson, 2002; Clark et al., 2003; Davies and Artaraz, 2009). There has been some resistance to or misunderstandings of the notion of 'pupil voice' in the development of practice and policy (Bragg, 2007) and Cook-Sather (2002, p. 5) has described the young as the 'missing voice' in educational research.

Since 2000, it has become more acceptable to include young children's perspectives of their experiences and their views are increasingly seen as being important to educational and social research (Holmes, 1998; Greig and Taylor, 1999; Lewis and Lindsay, 2000; Aubrey et al., 2000; Christensen and James, 2000; Eide and Winger, 2005; MacNaughton et al., 2007; Valentine, 2009).

Some lessons from recent studies include views that:

- exploring children's perspectives on their own learning can be illuminating;

- innovative approaches solve the methodological challenges (Burnett and Myers, 2002; Critchley, 2002; Marsh and Thompson, 2001).
- in the light of the United Nations Convention of the Rights of the Child (UN/UNESCO, 1989), the involvement of children as research *participants* rather than research *subjects* should be afforded them as a matter of right (Nutbrown, 1996).

Under the UN Convention children have the right to be consulted on matters which affect them; this clearly includes their preschool experiences. Tensions which can arise in 'voicing' children in research are the possibility of political manipulation of less powerful voices. If 'voice' research is an emancipatory act, there is an argument that in order that young children's voices are really heard and their viewpoints truly taken into account in the development of policy and the evolution of practices, their involvement needs to be fundamental, not superficial or tokenistic.

> Any study which seeks to include young children's perspectives must take issues of 'voice' as central to the methodology and find ways to 'listen' to those young voices and act on what they say. Though it will not always be possible to accommodate fully all the views and suggestions made by children, it is the case that many of the views that young children offer can often be incorporated into changes in practices and settings which make the place more inclusive and enabling for all who attend. (Nutbrown and Clough, 2009, p. 202)

The active listening undertaken by adult interviewers in this study provided an opportunity to 'turn up the volume' on young children's voices and to learn how they viewed practices and people in their preschool groups by asking the question: *How do 3–5 year old children experience their preschool settings?*

The study covered five regions of England (representing a geographical spread around England and settings ranging from rural counties to large cities), including a total of 18 preschool settings and 188 children. The sample of children interviewed included 93 boys and 95 girls aged between 3 years 2 months and 5 years 1 month. Children's ethnicity was described by the interviewers as: White British (104), Black British (9), Asian (6), Mixed Heritage (13). Details of ethnicity were missing for 56 children.

Questions to children were designed to find out how they most like to spend their time and what they thought of the equipment and experiences provided in the setting for them, and the relationships they formed with staff and other children. The children were very keen to talk about the things that they did, and what they liked, and gave informative responses. The adults who carried out the interviews worked in their preschools and so were known to the children, respected children's right to refuse to take part, and ensured that the children knew they could choose to stop at any point. Most interviews were in English, it being the first language of the majority of children interviewed, but in one setting two interviews were carried out in both English and Urdu because a member of staff in the setting spoke Urdu and the children were accustomed to using both languages.

Drawings are a useful means of understanding the perspectives of children and young people (Mauthner, 1997; Papatheodorous, 2002; Leitch et al., 2007; Griffiths, 2009). Following their interview, each child was invited to draw a picture of what they liked or disliked in their preschool setting and the interviewer made a note of what they said about their pictures as they drew. In all, 127 (68%) children chose to draw (57 boys and 70 girls). These drawings provided a means of collecting data through children's 'visual language' (Hall, 2009) and utilised what is known about the relationship between talking and drawing (Kress, 2000; Anning and Ring, 2004; Coates and Coates, 2006).

The major themes which emerged were:

- people;
- wishes;
- playing – outdoors and indoors.

Of the 188 children, all but five (2.7%) were emphatic that they liked going to their early years group. The five who expressed a different view (three boys and two girls aged between 4:1 and 4:7, attending five different settings) said:

'Yes, [I like nursery] but I do miss mummy sometimes.'

'No, I miss mummy.'

'No.'

'No.'

'I like it sometimes.'

Examples of comments from children who said they liked coming to their preschool included:

Yeah! I like playing in the house with the babies (dolls). (Mary, 3:7)

Yes – Two sands, two waters, even got a waterfall and the toast! (Leon, 3:3)

Yes, because it's fun at nursery but it's not fun at your house because you don't have anyone to play with only your mum, dad and your baby sister. (Ruby, 4:6)

Yes, I like snack and lunch, and did you write that I like digging in the sand outside? (Moses, 4:1)

All but seven (3.2%) of the 188 children interviewed said that they had friends in their preschool group (91 boys and 90 girls), with most (174, 93%) naming more than one friend. Seventy-five boys and 85 girls named their friends.

> *Billy, Jordon, Bobby, Michael – I've got lots of friends here.* (Lisa, 4:2)
>
> *Well, if I needed help I would ask a friend.* (Billy, 4:9)
>
> *Tim – and all of the boys and all of the girls.* (Bobby, 4:6)
>
> *Emmie – I always pick Emmie to do something.* (Lilly, 3:6)
>
> *With Elsa we play mums and dads. Elsa is the dad and I am the mum and then we swap over.* (Izzy, 4:4)

It was not uncommon for children to name both boys and girls with 156 (83%) children mentioning both boys and girls and seven boys only mentioning boys and nine girls only mentioning girls. Two boys and two girls said they did not have any friends. One said '*No, I just play by myself*' (Allun, 3:5).

Three children named staff as their friends. The children in this study listed 'playing', 'playing mums and dads', and 'playing football' as specific things they liked to do with their friends, with 'playing' being the most usual answer. Friends featured highly in the children's drawings as well as in their interviews. Of the 127 children who drew pictures, 52 chose to draw their friends.

Much has been written about the quality of relationships which adults create with the young children they work with (Elfer and Dearnley, 2007; Goldschmied and Jackson, 2004; Nutbrown and Page, 2008). The children in this study had a lot to say about the adults in their settings, and gave many different reasons why they liked them. All but 11 (177) children (94%) said that some of the grown-ups in their preschool were special: 165 (88%) named them, with 97 (52%) children naming more than one person. The children said they were special, giving such reasons as:

> *... cos I love you all! ... because she's kind ... she does cooking ... she's magic! ... she gives the best cuddles ... she's funny ... I like her hair ... she teaches us things ... she plays football ... he does drilling ... he is funny ... because they are my friends and play with me.*

Drawings featuring preschool staff included:

- 'Susie and me in the home corner.' (Figure 7.4)
- 'Bryonie with the babies and me helping.'
- Holly's friends.
- 'Bill drilling.'
- 'Shaun playing outside.'

Figure 7.4   'Susie and me in the home corner'

Children were also asked: 'Is there anything else you wish you could do here?' Of the 188 children in the study, 128 (68%) expressed a wish for something in their setting. Their wishes were wide-ranging and many were idiosyncratic, however top of the list were outdoors and popular culture.

The most popular requests centred around outdoor equipment, such as: a roundabout, swings, a truck that goes right up to the sky, a real pond with magic baby hippos in, playing more football, a real little house outside, trees to climb.

The second most popular set of wishes concerned aspects of new technologies and popular culture, with 20 children (11%) making suggestions such as:

> we need power rangers costumes and powers … I'd like to be Ben 10 in the house … transformers … I'd like to play on the Wii … I could bring my Nintendo … I'd like Cbeebies … I'd like music for dancing but no adults telling us the music or what we can sing.

Young children have their own distinct views and, given the right circumstances are able to express those views.

The children in this study have conveyed an emphatic message that:

- they mostly enjoy attending their early years groups;
- they have good relationships with the adults who work with them;
- their friends are important to them;
- they have many and varied suggestions for adding to or changing their preschool experiences.

The theme around friendships indicated the importance that these young children placed on relationships, with their peers and with the adults who worked with them in their preschool settings. If young children see their caring adults as important to them, this adds weight to the role of the *Key Person* in children's preschool lives (Goldschmied and Jackson, 2004; Elfer and Dearnley, 2007).

The children in this study have demonstrated that, though young, they have clear views about the places where they spend much of their time and that, given the opportunity, they are capable of expressing those views to interested adults. This 'participative ethos' is needed if what the children say is to be given 'due weight', according to the UN Convention, and their views are to be influential in change (Berthelsen and Brownlee, 2005).

Conclusion

Through a selective review of a series of small-scale studies and observations, this chapter has shown how including young children is multidimensional and how, with thought and careful planning, adults can develop practices and pedagogies which ensure that inclusion remains at the forefront of their work. The studies in this chapter demonstrate that inclusive practices are good practices and that benefits accrue for all. In the next chapter we shall examine how the inclusive agenda can be extended to parents.

Workshop 7 Including children

The studies presented in this chapter as examples of including children focus on a range of different issues: listening to babies and toddlers; key workers; meeting individual needs; planning outings; assessment; emotional intelligence and well-being; and playground friendships. These themes illustrate the breadth of opportunities that exist in almost every setting to review existing practices to ensure that children really are included.

Staff may wish to focus on one or two of the studies discussed in this chapter as a stimulus for reviewing, in discussion, how they maximise opportunities to include all children in their setting/service.

Policy points

Children's views are now features in government policy and, in line with the UN Convention on the Rights of the Child, governments consult children on matters that affect them. In a government-commissioned study to elicit views of children's experiences of the Early Years Foundation Stage Garrick et al. (2010) examined children's participation, involvement and engagement. They reported thus:

Exploring children's participation

'Despite some barriers, children in several settings exerted influence over everyday decisions about the content and direction of their play. This was often where the setting was less organised for specific play contexts and some spaces were left open to interpretation by the children, such as in the Steiner kindergartens.' (Garrick et al., 2010, p. 7)

Investigating children's involvement in planning

'Although children's interests were often cited by practitioners as informing their planning, it has been difficult to find clear examples of children being aware of this. However, some examples suggest that practitioners who vary the roles they take with children, and engage with play that children initiate, are better able to support and involve them with decisions about ongoing planning.' (Garrick et al., 2010, p. 7)

Examining the extent to which children's needs were met

- 'Children's comments suggested that their needs and interests were usually catered for;
- Children especially appreciated social play opportunities, social occasions and opportunities to care for others in their settings;
- Children's views reflected their need for parents, carers and siblings to be welcomed into settings;
- Children … talked about variations in how far adults get to know them as individuals;
- Children's comments suggested that in smaller settings, they were more likely to feel that adults knew them as individuals;
- Children demonstrated great interest in the rules, boundaries and routines of their settings. Some children seemed to find this structure helpful; others seemed to want more freedom;
- Children were often keen to understand why particular rules and routines were needed.' (Garrick et al., 2010, p. 2)

Concluding

'Although many of the findings reported here are consistent with themes, commitments and guidance in the EYFS, it was also clear that there are omissions in the EYFS, in part due to the emphasis on children as receivers of a curriculum generated by adults. The theme of children taking responsibility is one such omission which we have pointed to as evident in children's clear desire to engage with the world around them, to demonstrate their knowledge of the world around them and to maintain a range of types of relationships.' (Garrick et al., 2010, p. 8)

In England
The subsequent revision of the Early Years Foundations Stage states that:

'Providers must have and implement a policy, and procedures, to promote equality of opportunity for children in their care, including support for children with special educational needs or disabilities. The policy should cover:

- How the individual needs of all children will be met (including how those children who are disabled or have special educational needs, will be included, valued and supported, and how reasonable adjustments will be made for them);
- The name of the Special Educational Needs Co-ordinator (in group provision); arrangements for reviewing, monitoring and evaluating the effectiveness of inclusive practices that promote and value diversity and difference;
- How inappropriate attitudes and practices will be challenged;
- How the provision will encourage children to value and respect others.' (DfE, 2012, p. 26)

'The EYFS seeks to provide equality of opportunity and anti-discriminatory practice, ensuring that every child is included and supported.' (DfE, 2012, p. 2)

In Scotland
Four Key Principles apply:

- 'Rights of the Child
- Relationships
- Responsive Care
- Respect.' (Learning and Teaching Scotland, 2010, p. 8)

And

'The curriculum must be designed, managed and delivered to take full account of each learner's individual needs and stage of development. Designing the curriculum requires planning in partnership with young people, their parents and carers and with a range of others who can contribute effectively to their learning, based on good evidence of progress in learning'. (Scottish Government, 2008, p. 28)

'It will offer better educational outcomes for all young people and will provide more choices and more chances for those young people who need them.' (Scottish Government, 2008, p. 7)

In Northern Ireland
'When implementing personal development and mutual understanding schools should give priority to the needs of the child and provide a variety of activity-based learning experiences in support of these needs. They should ensure that each child feels valued.' (CCEA, 2007, p. 40)

In Wales
'Positive partnerships with the home are fostered and an appreciation of parents/carers as the children's first educators is acknowledged.' (WAG, 2008, p. 4)

Further reading

Field, F. (2010) *The Foundation Years: Preventing Poor Children Becoming Poor Adults. The Report of the Independent Review on Poverty and Life Chances.* London: HMSO. Available at: http://webarchive.nationalarchives.gov.uk/20110120090128/http:/povertyreview.independent.gov.uk/media/20254/poverty-report.pdf

Graham, A. (2011) *Early Intervention: The Next Steps – An Independent Report to Her Majesty's Government.* London: HMSO. Available at: www.dwp.gov.uk/docs/early-intervention-next-steps.pdf

Jackson, L. (2012) *Securing Standards, Sustaining Success: Report on Early Intervention.* London: National Education Trust.

Jones, P. and Welch, S. (2010) *Rethinking Children's Rights: Attitudes in Contemporary Society.* London: Continuum.

Nutbrown, C. and Clough, P. (2009) Citizenship and inclusion in the early years: understanding and responding to children's perspectives on 'belonging'. *International Journal of Early Years Education,* 17(3): 191–206.

Powell, J. (2005) Anti-discriminatory practice matters. In L. Abbot and A. Langston (eds), *Birth to Three Matters: Supporting the Framework of Effective Practice.* Maidenhead: Open University Press.

Including parents

"Just being involved helps children because it shows your interest in what they do and helps them to understand it is worthwhile." (Mother attending an accredited course on children's learning)

Introduction

In this chapter we will focus on issues of involving parents and the steps that need to be taken to ensure that all parents are included.

Parental involvement in the early years

The involvement of parents in their children's learning has long been established as an important element in early years provision. Margaret Macmillan, in the 1920s included 'lectures' for parents in her development of nursery schools. The establishment in the 1960s of the Preschool Playgroups Association by a young mother Belle Tutaeve marked the beginning of a more visible phase of parental involvement in their young children's learning. During the 1960s programmes to involve parents began to be developed – largely as a way of compensating for limited opportunities provided for some children at home. However, as currently understood, 'parental involvement' has some root in the Rumbold report, *Starting with Quality* (DES, 1990), which promoted the idea that parents were their children's first and most important educators and should therefore be involved in their early years learning experiences. Current government policy makes it clear that involvement with parents is an expected part of early childhood education and care in all settings:

> Parents are children's first and most enduring educators. When parents
> and practitioners work together in early years settings, the results have a
> positive impact on the child's development and learning. Therefore, each
> setting should seek to develop an effective partnership with parents. (QCA/
> DfES, 2008a)

As some recent examples have shown (Whalley, 1997; Draper and Duffy,
2001; Nutbrown, Hannon and Morgan, 2005), the model of parental
involvement is largely and characteristically *participative* – a far cry from
the *compensatory* ethos which dominated early programmes in the 1960s
and 1970s.

Throughout the 1990s, Sheffield Local Education Authority, among
many others, promoted partnership with parents in schools throughout
the city and these partnerships took many forms. Workshops aimed at
helping parents to support their children's literacy, open days to explain
the school curriculum, opportunities for adult learning and special
events to promote family learning were offered in many schools across
the whole age range from nursery to secondary.

In one school, for example, the 'Parents in Partnership' project led to the
development of a programme of accredited learning designed to help parents learn more about their children's learning in order better to support
them. An accredited course was designed for the parents, tailored to their
needs, with four units: sharing your child's school; sharing your child's
reading; sharing your child's maths; sharing your child's science. Parents'
comments confirmed the usefulness of the project and the aspirations of
many to continue lifelong learning. Some said:

> *I've got a greater awareness of child-centred learning and primary education.*
>
> *I think that it is easy to sit back and let school and teachers get on with doing
> their jobs but when I think back to when I was younger and how easy it was not
> to do any work, I want to help my child realise that learning could be fun.*
>
> *Just being involved helps children because it shows your interest in what they do
> and helps them to understand it is worthwhile.*

The headteacher of the school reported:

> A key aim is to raise achievement of pupils. Through being involved in the
> project parents can learn alongside their children and develop better under-
> standing of the expectations of school learning and there is shared understand-
> ing of where children's education is coming from and going to. Parents are
> continuing on their paths of *lifelong* learning too and many have yet to discover
> where those paths will lead. The potential is tremendous. (Firth, 1997, p. 97)

We are reminded here of our discussion in the opening of the book that
inclusion is not an *alternative* to raising achievement (see Ainscow et al.,

2004) but they are *co-terminous poles of the mission of social justice*. Hurst and Joseph (1998) argued for 'sharing education', the coming together of parents and practitioners in support of children's living and learning. They drew attention to the need for deep understanding of the complex cultural differences and shifts which children, parents and practitioners experienced when they entered each other's worlds and the opportunities for each to 'share' the others' experience. They warned:

> The sharing of intentions and perspectives between parents and practitioners is not easy in a busy classroom. There has to be a rationale for it, and it needs links with a curriculum model which sets a value on children's experiences at home with family and friends. It requires just as much commitment as sharing intentions with children does. Contacts with the home should be seen as a part of the curriculum, and a part of the practitioner's responsibility to provide for children's learning in ways that suit them. The first step is to consider what kind of contact with parents is most valuable, and to find out what kind of contact with the setting is needed by the parents. (Hurst and Joseph, 1998, p. 89)

Some initiatives to involve parents in the early years have focused on young children's learning or aspects of the curriculum and helping parents learn more about their children's ways of learning. In the late 1980s the *Froebel Early Learning Project* (Athey, 1990) identified ways of helping parents to understand their children's learning interests, or schemas, so that they could better support them. This theme was further developed by Nutbrown (2011), who argued that the more parents know about how children's learning developed, the better position they were in to understand what their children were doing and how they might further enhance learning opportunities for them. More recently, the PEEP Project (http://www.peep.org.uk) in Oxfordshire, has developed ways of involving parents with babies and young children in several aspects of their learning and development.

Settings and programmes continue to develop ways of working with parents in ways which are inclusive, participative, respectful and meaningful. Some settings have developed an international reputation for their work in involving parents in their children's learning, for example the Penn Green Centre (Whalley et al., 1997; Arnold, 2001), the Coram Children's Centre in London (Draper and Duffy, 2001) and the Sheffield Children's Centre. Most recently, Sure Start projects have involved parents in a range of programmes to support them in promoting babies and young children's health and physical, social, emotional and cognitive development. Weinberger, Pickstone and Hannon (2005) argues that listening to families was a crucial means of understanding how a particular Sure Start programme worked for them. Weinberger et al. (2005, p. 18) reports findings from a survey of parents of 4 year-olds, identifying the need for provision which meets various needs. One father mentioned the lack of facilities for men who were looking after their children, saying:

> ... if there's only one man and ten women with kids it doesn't seem to work. They ought to have father and toddler groups.

Many setting-specific projects have been developed to help parents learn more about their children's learning, such as that reported by Parker (2002), who explains how sharing work with parents on children's drawing and mark-making leads to enhanced understanding and enthusiasm from parents. Parker records the views of some parents who remarked:

> I have been able to enter her imagination and see the world through her eyes.

> Now I'm fascinated by the way she develops a drawing, rather than just looking at the end result.

> I have learnt that Brandon is more capable of mark making than I first thought. (Parker, 2002, p. 92)

Parker notes:

> The parents learned from observing their children and developed an appreciation of their children's high levels of involvement, discussing their children's achievements at home with confidence, clarity and joy. ... The children have been the primary beneficiaries of this collaboration between parents and practitioners. We all had valuable knowledge and understanding to share. This was a group which enjoyed mutual respect, shared understandings, political awareness and a commitment to extending learning opportunities for young children. (Parker, 2002, pp. 92–3)

Some initiatives to involve parents have focused specifically on the needs of minority groups, including families for whom English is not the language of the home. Karran (2003) describes work with parents who are learning English as an additional language and stresses the importance of bilingual support for such parents, who want to understand more of education systems and how to help their young children. Siraj-Blatchford (1994) has argued that in some cultures 'education' and 'home' are distinct and separate, and time may need to be given to explaining how home–school partnerships can support young children's learning and development. Baz et al. (1997) have discussed the importance of bilingual early childhood educators working bilingually with parents and young children using books, early writing, rhymes and poems in families' homes and in group settings.

The three year 'Making it REAL'[1] project in Sheffield and Oldham settings has identified meaningful ways of working in partnership with parents to support children's early literacy.

Practitioners' views on including parents

There is no doubt that much work is being done to include parents in their children's early years settings and to help them further support their children's learning and development. In the rapidly changing policy context across the UK, our research with small groups of early childhood professionals in a variety of disciplines, agencies and settings has involved life-historical interviews and focus group discussions to understand something of the impact of those policies as they are realised in the lives of early childhood professionals.

Practitioners' thinking on many of these issues may be influenced by other, international developments (some of which are becoming visibly manifest in practice if not featured in emerging UK policy development). Our study exposed some of the 'fine detail' of the agenda of multi-professional contexts of understanding and indicated that particular policies are differently interpreted in different ECEC contexts, with the key reason for such differences being:

- *Traditions of practice in types of settings*. What has been usual practice in, for example, a part-time voluntary-run play group has often been different from, say, the established practice of a nursery teacher in an LEA nursery class attached to a primary school.
- *Varied patterns and experiences of, and uneven access to, professional development*. Similarly, some voluntary-run, charity-based groups have in the past had different access to training opportunities. During the 1990s much training was policy oriented and little was devoted to discussing aspects of pedagogy. This is changing and the multi-professional nature of professional development is now an expected norm in many situations whereas this was a new phenomenon for many during the 1990s.
- *Personal beliefs and priorities*. In this rapidly shifting policy context of the UK, the personal life experiences of those who work with young children often drive their own priorities and expectations.

---

[1] See www.real-online.group.shef.ac.uk/makingitreal.html

Their discussions and interviews identified the following as important themes:

- *Adult involvement in children's learning.* Just how do adults get involved in children's learning? How should they involve themselves? How can they best support children's early learning and play?
- *Assessment.* Struggles over what and how to assess have occupied most early childhood practitioners. Issues of 'labelling' children early and of the burden of paperwork are concerns of many.
- *Children's rights.* Thinking about children's rights always raises debate. Not surprisingly, the participants in our study held a wide range of views on this topic.
- *Constructions of childhood.* Views of childhood as either 'vulnerable' or a time of discovery and challenge were discussed and, again, differing views led to interesting discussions. Can children really have 'rights'? Do 'rights' impact on how children are taught? Should practitioners consider issues of rights in their provision?
- *Curricula.* Just what should children be taught in this phase of learning? Different traditions emphasised different things, and some practitioners were strongly influenced by outside factors such as New Zealand's *Te Whariki* and the Reggio Emilia approaches to curriculum.
- *Equality.* Equality of access to preschool provision as well as equality in terms of teaching and learning opportunities was an important issue, and this linked very much to a discussion of inclusive practices.
- *Inclusive practices.* Some felt passionately about inclusive practices and views spanned the whole spectrum of the debate.
- *Parental roles.* Strong feelings and clearly expressed beliefs about parental involvement led to some lively discussions and there were one or two quite uncomfortable exchanges around these issues.
- *Play.* There were clear views on the importance of play, its place in the curriculum and providing for play in the context of current policies.

Practitioners spoke passionately about all of these and we learned from the focus groups that even though many used the same words and terminology, often they were intended to mean quite different things. So when people came together from different backgrounds language was crucial in allowing shared meanings to be developed.

Practitioners' positive beliefs and effective practices around parental involvement are, of course, crucial. Box 8.1 contains part of a transcript of an individual life-history interview which sheds light on one woman's feelings and actions in relation to parental involvement in her school.

Box 8.1 'Diane'

Text 2/excerpt 21

Peter Clough:	I think I may have/may have misunderstood that/do you mean that you'd/I mean if you were Headteacher, say/that you'd have open/I mean/just open access at all times/all times except?
Diane:	No/no except/no except/just/I mean tell me
PC:	those times when/those times when
Diane:	tell me what those times are/tell me when and when/when shouldn't a parent be with her child/his child/is there a time when
PC:	You just couldn't do it/I mean alright 20 children/that's maybe alright unlikely but you know/40 parents you just couldn't/you just couldn't *[laughing]* I mean practically...
Diane:	Peter you know you wouldn't have 40/and actually it would be 52 in my lot/my class/yeh you'd have times when it was/when it would be a lot/like lots but think what a message I mean what a message to parents like: this is our school/I am welcome there/no I belong there.

Text 5/excerpt 2

PC:	You said/it's there in the notes/you said 'When shouldn't a parent be with her child'/you have your own/your own children is that where that comes from/I mean something about your own being not welcome/being erm/excluded you know from their schools/erm settings
Diane:	No actually/no it's not that/I was always very welcome but then I was/I was/I had lots of things/lots of reasons to be included/but I was one of/oh a handful/a handful who actually bothered/oh shit I don't mean that other parents didn't bother/I mean didn't bother about their kids/god, no/but they didn't have the/the confidence to cross the doorstep threshold/didn't have
PC:	A sort of permission
Diane:	A sort of permission
PC:	I mean they couldn't permit themselves
Diane:	Oh I don't know about that/I don't know about/well

Text 5/excerpt 5

Diane:	My Dad was wonderful/he was a bugger of course but he was/he was/I love him he did everything/he did everything but everything I mean/new man in/what/1984, 85, 80s/he

(Continued)

(Continued)

	just loved us to death he was always there I mean he worked a/what? 50-odd hour week but/but actually it's him/I mean I love my Mum/my Mum was fabulous but it's Dad I remember as always being there/always being there/ always being there for us I mean with us, d'you know?
PC:	Well I know what
Diane:	But he never/I mean he never set a foot in our/in my school not once/not once/and Mum came only once/only honestly the once PC: '80s/well perhaps schools
Diane:	They had a fear of it/a fear of it just a simple fear of it which
PC:	To do with their own experiences
Diane:	they couldn't get over/perhaps not a fear/yeh to do with their/but/but look I don't think it's any different now/any different now/I mean any different now/we have a/we say come and read/come and/come and do woodwork or/or/ show us your stamps or something you know what I mean/ come and/but what if you can't read or do woodwork or/ or/have stamps you know/I mean do you have to have a reason like that/a reason a reason like that you know to/to/ get in there?

Text 5/excerpt 8

Diane:	You know the parents reading/the reading scheme we have with/well my Dad invented that *[laughter]*/I mean he used to ask/he used to say what have you/have you brought anything home to read with me/can we read/and we read/we read/we read/but he never set a foot in the school and why
PC:	Because
Diane:	And why/because it was the other side/the other of the tracks/the other/side of the tracks

Text 5/excerpt 10

Diane:	I used to long for them to come/I used to plead/I did I used to plead and there was one thing one event a/a concert/a Christmas concert well anyway/and I cried/I cried/I cried but they wouldn't come/there was one occasion just one occasion just one occasion when/when my Mum came/my Mum came and that was a /disaster
	[Silence]
	That was a disaster/I was so/ashamed of her/I was so/ ashamed of her
	[Silence]
PC:	Do you want to/shall we leave this/leave this for today

Diane: No/no/no/I/no/It's awful but when I see our parents/I mean when I see our parents/our parents here dragged along/it was a gym display my Mum came to/and she just stood and/stood and looked lost and/bitter somehow d'you know/looked sort of/scathing like she knew she didn't belong so she/so she/stood there/not there and she had her pride or/or something/and I wanted her to

Text 6/excerpt 2

PC: You're saying that things haven't changed/we haven't moved on since the

Diane: Oh they have of course they have/I mean we have policies we're/making the effort we've/got the badges and the banners but I know/I know when I/when I see them or I/don't see them I know/the other side of the tracks thing y'know/we're not/we're not/well the inclusion/that's another thing or the same thing/we're

Text 6/excerpt 17

PC: I'll go back/let me go back to that/d'you remember saying about/total access/always access/you remember that/well

Diane: Oh yeh/oh yeh/no question/open house/open house

Diane, like many, brings to her professional practice, her own more personal experiences as a young pupil. Other participants in the study gave their reactions to the following statements about parents' involvement:

As much involvement as possible as this gives parents a greater understanding of what is being achieved and then parents can reinforce these values in the home. (Montessori teacher in England)

Oh! Sometimes they just make it worse, I know that's a horrid thing to say, but if I could just get on with it sometimes, but some parents make me feel it's my fault their children behave so badly! I s'pose they don't mean to, and, well, one particular mother, she, well, she just has to get at somebody – so it seems that it's me. Wears you out though… (Nursery teacher in Wales)

Parents are their children's primary educators. I really believe that – they're not with us that long. Of course parents must be involved. (Playgroup worker in Northern Ireland)

The script in Box 8.2 is taken from a focus group exchange. Several focus group conversations on this theme were occupied with the dilemma of involving parents as a given 'good' and the realities of there always being some parents who apparently seek not to involve themselves, but who are, nevertheless, involved by virtue of being parents. Inclusion here was not primarily about the involvement of parents of children with learning difficulties or impairment, but about the inclusion of parents who were perceived as outsiders for other reasons – they smelled, drank excessively, were aggressive and so on. Some such parents fuelled a kind of resentment or dread in the hearts of some practitioners, as the following extract shows.

Box 8.2   'Mandy'

Mandy: There's this young woman, right, she's got a front tooth missing – probably her latest bloke knocked it out. She smells of sweat and stale lager, looks 35 but I think she's probably around 23. Two children – one just turned four – she's with us, and an 18 month-old. She doesn't want to 'get involved' – she just wants to hive off the older one all the time – thin little waif she is. And then she's in the pub every lunchtime say's she's no money – never has any money but manages to find her beer money. So, well… you can't really talk about parent involvement in their learning – not really, not when they're like that! And she's not only one – there are others.

Sue: Oh! But you can't say… you can't say they're all like that.

Mandy: A lot are though!

[Others are variously agreeing and disagreeing – Mandy's comment has allowed some difficult issues to surface.]

Sue: Well, it's a case of accepting that she's… she's …she's that little girl's mum, and she might have other difficulties but you can't ignore her…

Mandy: Easier said than done… I lose patience… When I see her coming I think – 'Oh my God, what's it going to be today?' … Find it really difficult – so hard to make an effort to involve her – because… well… I just don't feel comfortable around her. If I'm honest, I guess I'm saying… well… I just don't like her. I feel really sorry for the kids, and I think 'why can't you make an effort?' and I see other mums really struggling, but they do their hair and put on a bit of make-up and they wash their kids, now those, I'll do anything I can for them – ya know? Yeh? They've got to make an effort too haven't they?

[The group is silent and slightly awkward – no one speaks.]

Mandy: You all think this is a terrible thing to say – I can see…

This is difficult stuff. It was hard for Mandy to say and hard for the rest of the group to hear. But later we realised that Mandy had perhaps put into words the feelings of some other participants in the group. When the tape had stopped – others said to her that they understood what she was saying. They too sometimes resented those parents who seemed neglectful and they thought (not without guilt) that they treated such parents differently – perhaps making less effort to include them or have conversations with them about their children.

Such frank discussions were rare and highly sensitive, only occurring where a high degree of trust was established in the group. It is not possible to quantify the extent to which such views were held, but what emerged for some was the real feeling that it was, indeed, hard to include some parents whose lifestyles were at odds with generally accepted social norms within the community. What was also clear was the unshakable professional resolve that all parents should be included, whatever the personal feelings of practitioners. Including parents did not seem to be an issue where their children had learning difficulties, or if the parents themselves were disabled, or where parents were of different 'race', religion, or cultural heritage, or where their first language was different from that of the practitioners in the setting. 'Neglectful' parents, it seemed, were the hardest to include. It was particularly striking that, on the whole, practitioners held positive attitudes towards families whose children had learning difficulties and they talked about making particular efforts to make premises and events accessible and to offer time for discussion. What emerged from our discussions around parents was that some practitioners admitted that, though they tried to respond professionally, they were less likely to respond positively to parents who looked dirty and unkempt and behaved in ways which might, ultimately, put their children 'at risk', socially, emotionally or physically.

Participants who expressed such views expressed 'guilt' at holding such views and said that they made a conscious effort not to discriminate against such parents, but that they still felt that the parents they referred to as 'neglectful' and who seemed to regard their children as a 'nuisance' were the most excluded group.

Including parents – examples from practice

We conclude this chapter with a celebratory note: the three examples here show just what can be achieved when there is an ethos of inclusion which lies at the very heart of the work being undertaken. Box 8.3 outlines the Raising Early Achievement in Literacy Project and Box 8.4 explains how families and school staff come together as a learning community to celebrate learning journeys each term.

Box 8.3   The Raising Early Achievement in Literacy (REAL) Project

The REAL family literacy programme, developed and implemented by teachers at 11 schools, was 'long duration' (18 months) and 'low intensity'. It was based on a conceptual framework developed by Hannon and Nutbrown (1997) in which parents are seen as providing Opportunities, Recognition, Interaction and a Model of literacy (ORIM). The programme framework and examples of activities are fully reported (Nutbrown and Hannon, 1997; Nutbrown, Hannon and Morgan, 2005) and included five components:

- home visits by programme teachers;
- provision of literacy resources;
- centre-based group activities;
- special events;
- postal communication.

In these ways the programme sought to promote children's experience with family members of four strands of early literacy development: writing, reading and rhyming at home and greater awareness of environmental print. There was also an optional adult education component where parents were given information about local adult education classes and the opportunity to develop a portfolio of the work they had done with their child for accreditation. Details of the ORIM framework and programme evaluation, including literacy outcomes for children are given in Nutbrown, Hannon and Morgan (2005). An important element of the project was the parents' response to it. Without their involvement in it there would have been no project. When interviewed at the end of the project parents talked about how much more involved they felt in their children's literacy:

> I've loved being able to spend quality time to do these things with him, like painting, drawing and playing games. It's just sort of opened my mind that there are things you can do with them apart from sitting watching videos.

> It's been a big help actually. I do think Alan has learned a lot. It makes parents aware of the things they can do with children, because to be honest, especially when you have your first child, you're a little bit unsure.

> Now I know rhymes I can sing with the little one.

> It made me spend a lot more time with his older brother. I do a lot more reading with him; it's had a big impact.

> I got more ideas of things to do, like writing in sand and salt and environmental print.

> Sometimes Diane [a programme teacher] used to leave me little leaflets, things to look out for. I used to consciously observe Louise then, whereas perhaps I wouldn't have done before.

> Before I would have just opened a book. I probably wouldn't have prompted Julian as much as I do.

Take up for the programme was high (100%) and few left the programme. Two of the possible reasons for this were the inclusive nature of the programme; it was non-stigmatising and highly flexible:

> *A non-stigmatising programme.* The programme was non-stigmatising; it was not restricted to families who were perceived to be in the most need, for example, by including only those entitled to free school meals. Instead, families were randomly selected from all those whose children were the appropriate age on school waiting lists.

> *A highly flexible approach.* This was not a restricted family literacy programme, that is, parents were not obliged to undertake the adult education component. Indeed, only 10% chose to do so. Parents' interest in their own education may not always coincide with their being very ready to facilitate their children's development – making adult education a compulsory part of a family literacy programme may affect take-up and participation. Programmes must be flexible; home visiting makes it possible to tailor programmes to families' routines and literacy needs. In the current programme, it was possible to opt for evening home visits. In this way it was hoped to include as many families as possible, including those who were working. A high response to family literacy programmes can be expected if they reach out sufficiently; programmes must not rely on a restricted approach.

(Nutbrown et al., 2005)

As the REAL project illustrates, parents will 'vote with their feet' and choose not to participate in events and programmes or provision which do not meet their needs or include them as rightful participants. Where practitioners, parents and children work flexibly and respectfully together, everyone can gain from the experience.

It is important to be able to point to the rich benefits of including parents in celebrating their children's learning and achievements. To do this we draw, in Box 8.4, on the work of Robin Taylor, a reception class teacher who uses creative activities to include families in celebrating learning journeys.

Box 8.4   Relationships and participation (Robin Taylor)

Parental involvement is a value as well as a set of actions or activities and as such is something that has grown and gathered momentum within our practice and become inherent in our actions and thinking. It can be related to the wonders of Reggio and Te Whariki (New Zealand Ministry of Education, 1995), as well as the experiential educational approach of Ferre

(Continued)

(Continued)

Laevers (Laevers, 2002), and can even be found in the annals of government policy, such as Excellence and Enjoyment. Although this may not add kudos to the cause, it certainly reflects research findings by the likes of Kathy Sylva and the EPPE team.

For me, it came out of an evolving sense of what I should share with parents, a sense of togetherness, a sense of shared values through actions – and as the values were ones of creativity, celebration and collaboration, then only activities that would make visible the principles behind my practice and also implicitly refer to the 'weaving' inherent in the Te Whariki Early Childhood Curriculum, would be the ones with most validity – ones that had a feeling of 'exact rightness'. And the creative activities that we involved ourselves in were, like the Reggio Children so wisely say, inventions of things we hadn't thought of before, something that appeared by accident, through a series of experiences, interests and connections.

One summer I found myself at the WOMAD world music festival near London, and as I wandered around in the sunshine I came across a gigantic weaving frame that was being used to invite people to create together a collaborative woven structure made from reclaimed and recycled materials. There were families, children, friends and 'strangers' side by side, participating together, in what, I am sure, Kathy Sylva would have enjoyed calling 'sustained shared thinking'. All the participants, whether they were 5 or 55, were talking, helping, laughing, relaxing, sharing, enjoying and creating together; and, they were creating something that made that enjoyment visible, that made the values of 'collaboration', 'creativity' and 'celebration' palpable and lasting in that strange 'recycled and reclaimed' form of a woven mat.

At the end of the Autumn term 2004, the first term that young 4 and 5 year olds had spent together at Colston's Primary School, was a point in a journey that I felt should be celebrated. Here, I thought back to the woven structure I had seen at WOMAD music festival. I wanted a way of celebrating this journey together – a celebration that would invite all the important people in our lives to come together and mark the occasion – and what better way to do that but make a woven circle together, a circle of experiences, feelings, learning, lives and relationships. The values of the Te Whariki document – those principles and strands woven together in a symbolic Maori mat – were ones that I wanted to emulate. Family and Community, Relationships, Contribution, Communication, Exploration, Belonging and Well-being are implicitly inclusive and participatory. I wanted to emphasise the 'exact rightness' of our endeavour to create a sense of community within and beyond the classroom, to connect together the many worlds of children, their many communities and the relationships within them and throughout them, connecting together children, parents, teachers and families, and making these values explicit, and saying, 'Yes, we are on a learning journey together, in which all can contribute, in which all have a part to play, in which many perspectives have a place and in which everyone has a space'. So, we built a large frame from willow, a circle, to which we could weave together reclaimed materials that would represent our journey, our values and our time in our communal history, one that would act as a creative 'document' in our collective archive.

Figure 8.1 Every journey has a beginning – while weaving the willow circle we began to weave new ideas and principles into our practice

This initial collective endeavour to create alongside parents and children set a precedent and became a pattern in our practice, with weaving becoming a central form of how to make our values and principles explicit and intrinsic in our actions and thinking. We began a journey together, a creative one in which we wove new ideas and principles into our practice, while making this

(Continued)

(Continued)

visible by building large weavings to document that pedagogical journey of relationships, communication and participation.

The 'star' or 'sun' which we wove in the spring term not only emphasised the lengthening days and the change in seasons, but also the growth in our own learning, the learning of both children and adults. As educators, we were becoming more adept at understanding the importance of high levels of involvement and participation by parents, carers and families, with an emphasis on sharing values, theories, principles and how these may be carried through into practice. We began to outline the reciprocal relationships between theory and practice – how we all can offer multiple, conflicting or confluent perspectives, both local and international, both personal and academic. In this, the 'spring' of our journey, we were able to sew deeper threads of understanding into our 'educational weft', creating a strong mat, the strands of which were more richly understood. Parents, families, siblings, carers and teachers began to understand the significance of talking, creating and enjoying life at school together. These relationships enabled further communication, further dialogue among all the protagonists, and begun to be what Reggio so succinctly say, provocations for learning.

Creating structures for end-of-term celebrations means we are finding new ways of being, thinking, feeling, talking and acting together. We are, in our practice, creating that, 'a woven mat for all to stand on' (Carr and May, 1992, quoted in Carr and May, 2000, p. 59), upon which we invite all to stand – parents, children, teachers, families and communities – and we are attempting to create the levels of emotional well-being and involvement that Laevers states are fundamental to quality experiences in learning and living together, for children and adults.

When these 'Laeverian' values (involvement, openness and receptivity, vitality, relaxation, enjoyment without restraints), as well as communication, and thus relationships, are made explicit, it becomes self-evident that participation is invited, encouraged and provoked. However, it is important to stress that 'participation' is more than active involvement in the school – it represents a way of being, feeling, thinking and talking. Valentine states that:

> The reciprocal relationships that exist between child, family, school and indeed community are far reaching. To talk of a 'link' between the school and home is to undervalue what actually takes place in Reggio. In reality it is not so much that families take part in the life of the school but rather that, together with the children and the teachers, *they are* the school. (Valentine, 1999, p.11)

We are looking to emulate this value system and to capture the richness of children's lives and relationships with their parents and the adults and children at school and beyond. We want to construct experiences together with parents and families. In order to do this there is a recognition of the importance of both flexibility and robustness in our thinking and how that directly affects our practice. The weaving of reclaimed materials, the invitations to storytelling events, grandparents' tea parties, teddy bears' picnics in the park or withy weavings inspired by the work of Andy Goldsworthy, may be the 'visible' end of the involvement spectrum, but implicit within these collective creative activities with families are the values we imbue in them.

Figure 8.2   Where children, teachers and families feel at home – creating structures for end-of-term celebrations

Participation must be used as a starting point for a journey into the uncertainty of the future, a journey that must be collaborative and built upon trusting, loving, reciprocal relationships. Relationships and participation are about building a new pedagogical space that is always striving towards an education that is the best for children; but it is also much more than this because it represents a process of 'understanding life, and within life, education' (Balaguer, 2004, p. 32). If a common purpose is made apparent (that of constructing a better

(Continued)

(Continued)

school, society and world for children), then the power of relationships, the absolute necessity for all protagonists to be involved and the value of communication becomes paramount.

In order to create a 'woven mat for all to stand on' we must continue to endeavour to answer the fundamental questions of education, of our pedagogy and principles, to understand the importance of the rights of parents to 'participate actively, and with voluntary adherence to the basic principles, in the growth, care and development of their children who are entrusted to the public institution. This means no delegating and no alienation. Instead, it confirms the importance of the presence and role of parents ...' (Malaguzzi, 1995, p. 68). Not only must we endeavour to do this through active involvement in collective creative activities, but with explicit dialogue about an 'effective shared search for the best educational methods, content and values' (ibid., p. 69). And we must make this communication open, honest, reciprocal and explicitly inclusive and participatory. And when I see three generations of the same family come together on a Teddy Bears' Picnic, to sing, play, story and, later, celebrate the learning journey of their daughter and granddaughter by looking at photographs and documentation of our year at school (alongside other parents, children, families, as well as office staff, caretakers and teachers and other practitioners), I see the values of Family and Community, Relationships, Contribution, Communication, Exploration, Belonging and Well-being made visible, strong and woven together with the nurturing and respect of children and their families.

In the following example (Box 8.5) we can see how the strengths and talents of parents can be used to support the learning of staff, and how a community activity can bring many families together in common purpose.

Box 8.5   Vegetable garden

The nursery was developing their practices on sustainability. This was a decision taken by staff, following a very dry spring, when the children had been talking about running out of water in the small pond in the well landscaped nursery garden. This setting had established practice in working with children outdoors with extensive outdoor play opportunities using logs, loose materials for den making and other constructions, making homes for animals such as hedgehogs and other beings, such as 'fairies, elves and friendly monsters'.

The initiation of a vegetable garden was a challenge for the staff; none was a gardener, none had grown vegetables themselves. They had already enlisted the support of three fathers to make some raised beds for the children to plant vegetables. They were advised that this was easier for the children to manage.

It became clear that the gardening project had to be one of mutual learning. One of the families had an allotment, where everyone in that family was involved. The father (a lone parent) took his two daughters (aged 3 and 7) to the allotment almost every weekend where they enjoyed time together preparing, digging, planting, watering, weeding, harvesting ... whatever the season needed. In the allotment shed, the two girls also enjoyed eating their packed lunch and playing with the toys they brought from home.

It was only when the 3 year old told her teacher that they had an allotment that the staff realised that they would be wise to use the knowledge, skills and enthusiasm of this family to get the gardening project really going, and to enthuse others. The invitation went out, asking families to help, and the vegetable garden project took off.

One parent fixed a water butt with a crate early to store small watering cans, another organised the delivery of compost. Staff and children decided what to plant, taking advice from gardening parents about what grew well and were less susceptible to slugs and snails and likely to yield something that could be harvested and eaten by the children. Buying the right tools and a set for adults to use was important too.

Weekend and holiday care of the garden was an issue to be resolved. The family with the allotment couldn't take this on (because they had their allotment), but other families who had discovered the pleasure of gardening vegetables as a result of involvement in the project got involved, and in a sense the nursery vegetable garden became a community family allotment.

The new shed contained tools, seeds, pots and so on, and several sets of keys were cut for parents who were happy to pop down and do a little work and watering when the nursery was closed.

The garden belonged to the families. There were difficulties and tensions along the way, and as issues arose the solutions had to be worked out, but on the whole the sense of belonging which was created outshone the difficulties.

Conclusion

In this chapter we have highlighted the tradition of 'parental involvement' as a contribution to the inclusive culture of early childhood settings. We have shown how several successful research studies include parents as an essential component.

Workshop 8 Including parents

For some practitioners, their beliefs, values and practices on including parents in Early Childhood Education and Care provision are influenced by their own experiences as children. Some parents are able to include themselves – others, for whatever reason, are difficult to include.

Staff may wish to use this chapter to stimulate discussion on their own policy and practices on including parents. They may wish to review what they do in the context of their definitions of inclusion developed in earlier workshops and identify ways of reducing any existing barriers (personal, practical, institutional) to the inclusion of parents in their settings/services.

Policy points

Across the UK, policies pay attention to the involvement of parents in their children's learning and development. Though differently expressed, they all concur that parents are central to children's lives and learning.

In England
'Parents and/or carers should be kept up-to-date with their child's progress and development. Practitioners should address any learning and development needs in partnership with parents and/or carers, and any relevant professionals.' (DfE, 2012, p. 10)

The Early Years Foundation Stage 'seeks to provide partnership working between practitioners and with parents and/or carers.' (DfE, 2012, p. 2)

Providers must make the following information available to parents and/or carers:

- How the EYFS is being delivered in the setting, and how parents and/or carers can access more information (for example, via the DfE website);
- The range and types of activities and experiences provided for children, the daily routines of the setting, and how parents and carers can share learning at home;
- How the setting supports children with special educational needs and disabilities;
- Food and drinks provided for children.

In Scotland

Self-evaluation encourages staff to consolidate their thinking in relation to:

- The specific needs and interests of every baby or young child;
- Progress relating to all aspects of children's development and learning;
- Communication with parents;
- The ways in which the environment meets the needs of all.

'Inclusion and responsive care are crucial if children's rights are to be promoted effectively. Through working closely with parents and other professionals, staff in early years settings recognise that all those involved with children and families have an important contribution to make.' (Learning and Teaching Scotland, 2010, p. 20)

'Adults, including staff and parents, should have a shared understanding of, and commitment to, the need for ongoing observations in supporting and promoting children's learning and development.' (Learning and Teaching Scotland, 2010, p. 43)

'All children and young people have an entitlement to a curriculum which they experience as a coherent whole, with smooth and well-paced progression through the experiences and outcomes, particularly across transitions. Those planning the curriculum have a responsibility to plan, in partnership with others involved in learning, how they will jointly enable children to move smoothly between establishments, building on prior learning and achievement in a manner appropriate to the learning needs of the individual.' (Scottish Government, 2008, p. 17)

In Northern Ireland

'Throughout the Foundation Stage children need to be observed closely so that information can be shared with parents.' (CCEA, 2006, p. 6)

'Children learn best when a multi-professional approach exists and practitioners access the expertise of other professionals.' (CCEA, 2006, p. 4) (The acknowledgement of parents' expertise in regards to their own child is omitted.)

'It is important that children are supported by trained, enthusiastic and committed professionals who work in partnership with parents and carers and, where appropriate, professionals in other fields, to ensure that all achieve their full potential.' (CCEA, 2007, p. 9)

In Wales

'Positive partnerships with the home are fostered and an appreciation of parents/carers as the children's first educators is acknowledged.' (Welsh Assembly Government, 2008, p. 4)

Further reading

Guasp, A. (2011) *Different Families: The Experiences of Children with Lesbian and Gay Parents*. London: Stonewall/Education for All.

Nutbrown, C., Hannon, P. and Morgan, A. (2005) *Early Literacy Work with Parents: Policy, Practice and Research*. London: Sage.

Stonewall (2010) *Including Different Families*. London: Stonewall/Education for All.

Wheeler, H. (2009) *Parents, Early Years and Learning: Parents as Partners in the Early Years Foundation Stage*. London: National Children's Bureau.

Including staff

Introduction

"We're the last to know anything. The other day this mum came in and said 'What's this about the trip?' And I felt really stupid because I didn't know what she was talking about. I had to say that – and then find out. The mum looked at me gone out! I felt like an unnecessary spare part. Communication – it's an important thing. All staff need to know stuff like that – not just those in charge."
(Mary, Part-time nursery nurse in a Foundation Stage Unit in England)

Having argued the importance of including young children and their families in early years settings, we turn now to the third element of this important triangle of living and learning – the practitioners who work with families and young children. In this chapter we first consider various practitioners' definitions of inclusion and then move on to demonstrate how various inclusive projects can be used to develop inclusive strategies which ensure that, alongside children and parents, the staff too feel included.

In order successfully to promote inclusive practices, we need to understand what precisely is meant by the term. For, as we have said earlier, many consider 'inclusion' to be the latest in a series of terms used to refer to disabled children, children with impairments and learning difficulties and, particularly, those in mainstream settings who have been identified as having special educational needs. But inclusion is *not* the latest term for SEN, it has a different and much more comprehensive and socio-political meaning. As Booth (2000) puts it:

> Some continue to want to make inclusion primarily about 'special needs education' or the inclusion in education of children and young people with impairments but that position seems absurd. ... If inclusion is about

the development of comprehensive community education and about prioritising community over individualism beyond education, then the history of inclusion is the history of these struggles for an education system
which serves the interests of communities and which does not exclude
anyone within those communities. (p. 64)

Tony Booth's position here, then, is that inclusive education is about
education for *all* members of the community – and that embraces all
minority and oppressed groups. From this broad definition of inclusion
it could be argued that Sure Start initiatives and Early Excellence Centres
are, in effect, projects of inclusion in the early years. Weinberger et al.
(2005) document the developments in one Sure Start programme,
demonstrating that meeting expressed needs within a community can
create a dynamic whereby options are offered rather than being seen as
a 'take it or leave it' response to programme development for families.

   In a study carried out in 2002 we asked five early childhood educators
what they meant by the term 'inclusion'. Here they talk about their own
understanding of inclusion and what their settings do to develop inclusive practice.

> *It's about letting children with Special Educational Needs come to the school in
> their neighbourhood. I think that's right, but it doesn't always work out.* (Kay,
> nursery nurse, Nursery Centre 2–5 years)

> *It's political. It's about social justice – giving every child the right to an education
> in their own community – which enables them to reach their full potential. For
> me, that means doing a lot of work to make sure that the staff here is aware, but
> also arguing for resources. Managing that is a challenge. The greatest need is for
> personal awareness – so I need money for staff development. Installing ramps is
> easy; changing attitudes, challenging prejudice – that's the real issue of inclusion.
> It is a huge issue.* (Sue, headteacher, School 3–10 years)

> *Well, I think inclusion is really about equality. About not shutting children out.
> If children are kept out of the system at this stage they'll always be different –
> seen as different. It's easy to say that though – not always so easy to include
> children, especially some who are very disruptive. Children with disabilities aren't
> a problem – I don't worry about them – they usually fit in well – toilets are a
> problem sometimes but we get round that! It's children who can't behave, can't
> fit into the group, mess up the equipment, slop paint everywhere, throw things,
> bite – I tear my hair out over them. They're the ones that are in danger of exclu
> sion and being separated off at 5 years old. That's terrible, isn't it? But I can't
> help it – I have to survive, and I have to think about the rest of the children.*
> (Helen, reception class teacher, School 3–7 years)

> *A lovely idea – inclusion – and when it's good, it's great! I have been able to have
> children in the nursery with Down's Syndrome and children with various emo
> tional difficulties – abused children – but when they [the LEA] asked us to take
> in a child with autism, well, we had to say 'no'. Too risky – I was frightened that*

if we did, something terrible would happen and it would be my responsibility. So yes, lovely idea, but it really is an ideal that will never be achieved – total inclusion is impossible. (Janie, nursery teacher, School 3–10 years)

I spend my life arguing for extra support for children with SEN who we're trying to keep in our school rather than send them to 'Special'. Inclusion of all children in the community would be so much easier if it were the norm – the first resort – that's usually the case in the nursery, but as children go on into school that philosophy seems to fade and the first move seems to be 'How can I get rid of this one?' (Pauline, SENCO, School 3–10 years)

(*Source*: Clough and Nutbrown, 2002, p. 1)

So, how typical are these practitioners' voices on inclusion? To what extent can the political ideal of social justice be realised in practice in the early years of education? How far are these *ideals of equity* and *fears of risk* shared by early childhood educators generally? Wolfendale (2000) published a set of 'snapshots of practice' which includes many examples of work with children with special educational needs in the early years. The collection demonstrates the diversity of experience and attitude towards *needs* and to the concept of *inclusion*. Wolfendale presents many positive accounts of including young children with identified learning needs in nurseries or other early education settings and her book provides testament to the positive attitudes of practitioners to include all young children. However, there is another side to the coin – as our interviewees alerted. The failure of inclusion hurts. Nutbrown (1998) gives an account of a nursery teacher who, against her own honest and sensitive judgement, tried to include a child with autism into her nursery; things went badly wrong because of endemic difficulties within the setting itself (see Box 9.1).

Box 9.1 'Martin'

Martin was admitted to a nursery full of children with damage and dislocation in their lives – physical and sexual abuse, overwhelming poverty, disproportionate ill-health, numerous wet beds, and no end of broken hearts.

Martin stayed for two weeks. Each day his teacher talked with his mother. Each day she told her what Martin had enjoyed, and of the struggle he had with his peers in the nursery. There were many troubled children in Martin's company, and though Martin was interested, bright and he was able, the nursery disabled him. In that setting he was not being included in a calm, ordered society. He was not a member of a predictable community; he was appended into a community of children and adults in chaos.

(Continued)

> *(Continued)*
>
> After two weeks Martin left. His teacher hoped he had not been harmed, but she knew the harm it had caused his mother. Martin went to a nursery a few miles away which had a special unit for children with special educational needs and which worked to include children from that unit into mainstream classes once they had become established in the school community.
>
> (*Source*: Nutbrown, 1998, p. 170)

Martin's story is a warning that early years settings must be fit to include, and educators equipped with appropriate professional development and management support. It is perhaps also, and more subtly, an example of how the practitioner herself (not to mention her colleagues) was not fully included in the inclusion process in this case. Her views and responses were – to an extent – overridden by others who were intent on pursuing the inclusive agenda for children with special educational needs. And because this was an agenda that this teacher wanted to support, her own professional judgement in this case was ignored. Berry's (2001) study of four children with autism indicates that inclusion *can* work for some children with learning difficulties, and the factors for success depend upon the children's responses as well as those of educators and parents. Importantly, the ability of the adults to listen, really listen, to the children's voices and the voices of all practitioners involved is crucial.

How do we know inclusion when we see it?

The *Index for Inclusion* was first published in 2000 (Booth et al., 2000) and issued to all schools in the UK. A second edition was published in 2002 (Booth et al., 2002) followed, in 2004, by a specially adapted version for use in early years and childcare settings:

> In the *Index*, inclusion is an approach to education and childcare according to inclusive values, rather than a concern with a particular group of children and young people. Inclusion is often seen to be associated with children and young people who have impairments or are seen as 'having special educational needs'. However, in the *Index* inclusion is concerned with increasing the participation of all children as well as adults. We recognise that some children may be more vulnerable to exclusionary pressures than others and argue that settings should become responsive to the diversity of children and young people in their communities. (Booth and Ainscow, 2004, p. 1)

The *Index* takes a broad definition of inclusion, stressing participation of *all* children and not just the inclusion of a single group (such as children identified as having special educational needs). The *Index* seeks to support practitioners in developing their own responsiveness (and the responsiveness of the systems in place in the setting) to the diversity of children in those learning communities. The *Index* is summarised as follows:

> The *Index* is a set of materials to guide schools through a process of inclusive school development. It is about building supportive communities which foster high achievement for all students. The process of using the *Index* is itself designed to contribute to the inclusive development of schools. It encourages staff to share and build on existing knowledge and assists them in a detailed examination of the possibilities for increasing learning and participation for all their students.
>
> The *Index* involves a process of school self-review on three dimensions concerned with inclusive school cultures, policies and practices. The process entails progression through a series of school development phases. These start with the establishing of a co-ordinating group. This group works with staff, governors, students and parents/carers to examine all aspects of the school, identifying barriers to learning and sustaining and reviewing progress. The investigation is supported by a detailed set of indicators and questions which require schools to engage in a deep, and challenging exploration of their present position and the possibilities for moving towards greater inclusion. (Booth, Ainscow and Kingston, 2006, p. 2)

Use of the *Index* is, arguably, a fine example of collective and collaborative action research. Central issues include:

- the language and what individuals *mean* by the term *inclusion*;
- identification of *barriers to play, learning and participation* and identification of ways of reducing discriminatory attitudes and practices and institutional barriers;
- resources to support play, learning and participation within learning communities as a key factor and the need to mobilise resources and maximise use of human resources, including children and their parents;
- support for diversity – ways of using support which increases the capacity of the whole setting rather than only identifying support for specific individuals.

Additionally, the *Index* comprises four key 'elements' to support thinking about inclusive development: key concepts; a planning framework; review materials; and an inclusive process. The planning framework in the *Index* supports a structured approach to review and development, and suggests ways of working on creating inclusive cultures, producing inclusive policies and evolving inclusive practices. Materials are provided to enable a detailed review of all aspects of a setting and help to identify and implement priorities for change. These materials can make useful survey instruments in themselves as a way of 'taking the pulse' of inclusion within a setting. Using the *Index* is an inclusive process to ensure that the processes of review, planning for change and putting plans into practice are themselves inclusive. Young children, parents, staff and others associated with the provision are included in the process. Key, of course, is the question as to if and how using the *Index* makes a difference and how that difference influences the way practitioners work for inclusion.

So, the *Index* is intended to enable settings to 'sample' their cultures, policies and practices to see how they measure up to the view of inclusion articulated above by Tony Booth, a view which embraces inclusion of *all*, and addresses aspects of inclusion which we have identified throughout this book: gender, class, culture, 'race', religion, sexuality, and social class as well as learning difficulty or disability.

We know from our research that many early childhood settings and providers have not encountered the *Index*. Because of the diversity of provision, some settings may have missed the *Index*, and have not (as yet) been able to work with it or judge its usefulness to their settings.

Some Local Education Authorities and some schools have used the *Index for Inclusion* to great effect as an instrument of school change (Clough and Corbett, 2000). But we were interested in how the *Index* made a difference to individual professional responses to inclusion. We wanted to know whether using the *Index* affected the personal 'routes to inclusion' of early childhood educators. We wanted to know how *included* members of staff felt themselves and what they felt their role in inclusion was and how they could be supported – included – in developing inclusive practices. After they had used the *Index* in their own settings we returned to the five early years practitioners in our study and asked them to reflect on their experience, and to talk about their own learning. Of the *Index* they said:

> *Fantastic – a real eye opener. I never thought about some of the dimensions as being part of inclusive practice. I realise how inclusive we are! Of parents, of children from ethnic minority groups. It made me think 'Am I being inclusive – as a professional?' Yes, I've really learned quite a bit about me and my own attitudes, and about what other people who work here know too and have shared.*
> *(Kay, nursery nurse, Nursery Centre 2–5 years)*

> *It suggests setting up a co-ordinating group. That's important for large schools but it works equally well in small settings where there are not large numbers of staff. We used it in a series of staff meetings. Got the children as well as staff to do questionnaires. It really raised awareness, amongst staff, children and also with parents. My Governors were interested too – even when it came to spending*

money! There's very good practice – and positive will. It is such an effective process – takes some sustaining though! We were encouraged to realise that we had many aspects of inclusive culture and our main task was to extend and develop what we did. (Sue, headteacher, School 3–10 years)

When they said we were going to do this I thought 'another initiative in another glossy folder'. I was sceptical, I admit. I wondered what the point was of doing another audit when we could have spent the time and money on a part-time support assistance for my class. But it was interesting – made me think – but whether it will make a difference in the end, well, we'll see. (Helen, reception class teacher, School 3–7 years)

I learned loads just by reading through the folder, thinking about the questions posed under the different dimensions. There's so much to think about – mind-blowing! It's a process that's never actually finished, but it feels very good. It is really about developing relationships – that's what it's about – valuing people enough to make relationships with them and then finding ways of working in that richness of diversity. (Janie, nursery teacher, School 3–10 years)

He [the Head] said 'We should do this – take it home and see what you think'. As I worked through it, it all made sense – cultures, policies and practice – really obvious but it had to be laid out for us. So I took the folder back and said 'Yes – good idea – we should do this.' And the Head said 'Great! Will you set up the group?' It's been a lot of work but getting the children involved and the parents was really good – made a difference to the way we think about things now, I think. I would say that we're – most of us – at the point where we 'think' inclusion now – first. (Pauline, SENCO, School 3–10 years)

(*Source:* Clough and Nutbrown, 2002, p. 3)

We have been at pains here to let the voices of those people we interviewed speak for themselves, to convey – largely unedited – their experiences, excitements and reservations. But is such an *Index* necessary? It seems that it is not uncommon to greet yet another development initiative with scepticism, as Helen said: '*another initiative in another glossy folder*'. Yet the five people we spoke to have conveyed something of a personal response to the *Index*, which suggests a change *in themselves*. We are left with the impression that there is a great deal of personal interrogation, personal learning, personal change which results as an outcome of engaging with the *Index*. As Pauline said: '*we "think" inclusion now*'. Can such changes in thinking, in attitude, in realisation fail to result in changes in practice? If our five participants are in any way typical, we have something to learn about the capacity of the *Index* to bring about personal/professional change. As Kay told us: '*That whole idea that "inclusion" isn't just the latest PC term for SEN – that was really refreshing.*'

A key point in the interviews was the development of a shared language for discussion. Sue commented: '*We've got a language now to discuss things within the school*', and this change in language resulted in

Pauline negotiating a change in her title as Special Educational Need Co-ordinator:

> *I've asked to be called the 'Learning Support Co-ordinator' now. It doesn't really fit, being a SENCO in an inclusive school!*

Their work with the *Index* in their settings, they told us, made a difference to them as individuals. It was not always easy, as Helen admitted: '*It was painful at times. I had to confront and admit some personal prejudices.*' But it seems that these early childhood professionals would want to recommend the *Index for Inclusion* to others in other settings so that they can find out for themselves.

> *It's not something you can get second hand – you have to be part of the thinking, part of the change.*

As part of their work with the *Index for Inclusion* the practitioners in our study felt more included in the policy making, which evolved new and refined practices in their settings. Working together through the various themes of the *Index* meant that all staff were included in decision making and were able to make a contribution as informed participants in their settings. Inclusive practices were not imposed upon them; rather they were created by them as part of a shared and self-consciously critical process of professional development.

We carried out a small follow-up study in June 2005 to find out if the five practitioners in our study had been using the early years version of the *Index*. We were unable to locate Pauline, who had moved overseas to teach, but we were able to talk with her four fellow participants, all of whom were still working in the settings where we carried out our original study. Kay, now an advanced practitioner with responsibility for inclusive practice, told us: '*Yes, I was so pleased to find it. It's much more tailored to early years settings. I like the emphasis on play.*' Sue, still head-teacher of a primary school, remained firmly fixed on her social justice agenda. She told us: '*It has given us a new impetus. Great to have the early years language – I need both – but the focus on play is really welcome.*' Jane had been pleased to find the new version of the *Index* because she was now the leader of a new Foundation Stage unit in her school and said:

> *It's invaluable – gives ways of really taking parents with you, listening to what they want, what they believe. Creating a new environment here for everyone was quite a challenge so I've been using the framework in the* Index *to really find ways of developing an inclusive setting.*

Helen had just returned from 12 months on maternity leave, so she had yet to come across the *Index*. Perhaps we can learn from these practitioners that working *for*, *on*, *with* inclusion is a life-long commitment which means that 'inclusion' is never quite (or even anywhere near) 'done'?

The expectation of inclusive early years provision places high demands on practitioners who need to be supported in their work through appropriate professional development opportunities and opportunities to share and discuss their complex work. The following extract demonstrates the importance of support for staff who face difficult and emotionally challenging situations on a daily basis. Practitioners need to be allowed – from time to time – to admit to their own humanity and vulnerability and their own struggles to 'be' inclusive, as did Sharon when she told us:

> I can't always do it easily, but when I find myself 'closing off' people, parents, other staff even, then I think 'How would you feel, Sharon? How would you feel if you were left out?' I try to put me in their place and, well, bring them in – it's only right!

We could ask is anyone ever fully inclusive? Is it realistic to expect (or assume) that practitioners may not – from time to time – experience some difficulty in including 'this' parent or 'that' child? Perhaps it is only fair to acknowledge that, although they *practice* inclusion, there are times when inclusion costs practitioners – emotionally, physically, professionally. And so, for this, they need support.

Inclusion – a personal perspective

As part of our study of inclusive attitudes and practices we asked participants in our study to locate themselves along what we called an 'Inclusive Continuum'. We gave them the following exercise and, having placed their *x* on the paper to represent their position on the continuum, we asked everyone in the group to stand along a line which we had placed on the floor.

Box 9.2 How inclusive are you?

How 'inclusive' are you? Plot your own personal commitment to inclusive education on the following line. You need to decide where you – in a personal/professional role – stand on the continuum below.

Point A represents the view that everyone should be **included** in mainstream education settings and no child should be excluded – for whatever reason.

(Continued)

(Continued)

Point Z represents the view that *some* children may necessarily need to be ***segregated*** from mainstream settings.

A–B–C–D–E–F–G–H–I–J–K–L–M–N–O–P–Q–R–S–T–U–V–W–X–Y–Z

Inclusion   *Segregation*

Our research participants told us that they were quite happy to place their private *x* on their own anonymous sheet of paper but, when they took their place somewhere around the E, F, or G point on the scale, some said that they found it hard to 'admit' [their word] that they did not see themselves as 'fully inclusive'. No one in our study placed themselves at point A. Two people placed themselves at point B, explaining:

> *You have to allow – I mean you really have to allow that it may not ultimately be possible to... to have what? Severely multiply disabled, er bedridden and er wholly uncommunicative children in inclusive settings. That's just real, isn't it?*

And

> *I am utterly, just utterly, for inclusion. You can ask anyone – I'll do ten rounds with anyone on inclusion. But I think that where parents choose a separate, like a segregated, setting you're on a losing wicket. I mean why even try if you're fighting the child's best friends? Then you've got to go with supporting them, the parents, I mean.*

Of the 33 people in the group, 23 placed themselves around various clusters. People in the EFG cluster said things like:

> *I'm strongly for inclusion, but it's got to be in the child's best interests. I know some special schools which are actually more inclusive than our local comp, which makes such a fuss, a big banner-waving fuss, about how inclusive it is. So for me any reservation is not about a child's difficulty or whatever – those can be overcome with resources – but it's about the spirit – yes, the spirit – of the setting. Not what's wrong with the child, but is everything OK about the setting?*

> *You can't argue philosophically or politically with inclusion – I mean that's like arguing about breathing, isn't it? It's just natural. What isn't natural is squeezing square pegs into round holes when what's wrong is not the squareness of the pegs but the roundness of the holes... Does that make sense? I just mean that schools and settings need to be better places for it to work. I think in my work I'm, well, fighting for that. Do you know what I mean?*

The eight participants who placed themselves around the MNO cluster made comments such as:

> I feel a bit bad being down here. It's just, well, it's practicality stuff – staff = support – back up. Confidence I guess.

> It's not where I want to be. It's where I think I am in the place I work... Know what I mean, like?

> I think I'm just not good at SEN work. Maybe I'm scared. It might be experience. I've never – I've never worked with SEN children....

One person placed himself at the W point on the scale. He said:

> I worked in an inclusive school once – nightmare. Got attacked – hospital – the lot. Couldn't call it education. ... And the kids were young! But out of control. And the parents!!! Sorry – bad position – but if you've been bitten once....

The activity in Box 9.2 was a useful tool for collecting data from participants about their personal 'degrees of inclusion'. It is also, however, an effective tool for personal/professional development for practitioners in settings where there is a need to develop deeper understanding among the team as to where individual team members 'stand' on the inclusion continuum. The position practitioners choose for themselves on the continuum can be indicative of necessity – perhaps they feel that their current professional contexts dictate a particular inclusive/exclusive position, or their position on the line may be a statement of their own personal value position derived from a self-reflective and honest appraisal of their own moral/political position. For the participants in our study, both reasons were apparent across the group.

Part of the process of including staff involves making explicit what inclusion *is*. We used the exercise in Box 9.3 with groups of participants to stimulate discussion in focus groups on what was (and was not) an inclusion issue.

Box 9.3   Identifying inclusive issues

Think about the inclusive issues that have arisen in your own setting and then consider the following questions of inclusion.

Parental involvement

The majority of parents involved in a setting are mothers. Is there an 'inclusive/exclusive' issue here?

(Continued)

(Continued)

Bi/multilingual families

A family speaks three languages (other than English) and communication between parents and staff is limited because the staff speak only English. Is this an 'inclusive/exclusive' issue?

Travelling families

Three children of travelling families move into the area. The setting has already allocated all its places in the nursery and reception classes. The families are told that their children can have places in a school 1½ miles away which has spare places. Are there any 'inclusive/exclusive' issues?

Lesbian parents

A lesbian couple are foster parents to two young sisters (aged 2 and 4). Might there be any 'inclusive/exclusive' issues?

In response to the above themes, participants discussed at length issues of the gender of parents, home languages and travelling families. The following comments are indicative of the wide range of responses:

> *It is important to be aware of gender, and of the implications of parents' gender on their participation in events and things. Fathers are often sidelined in pre-school settings because they don't sort of fit and the things on offer don't really appeal to them. I think we've got work to do here to make sure they can feel like they belong too.*

> *People in England forget that, on a world scale, it's odd to only speak one language. We really should make more use of families who speak different languages. It's wrong that it's seen as a problem – bilingualism is a rich resource.*

> *It's a culture and a way of life that is traditional and deserves respect. Travellers are a minority group – yeah – but they have a way of life and ways of doing things that go back hundreds of years. We're ignorant of their traditions. That's why I think travelling families are sometimes seen as a problem, but again, we should see it as adding to the culture, not being a problem to solve.*

> *It will be important to ensure that activities in the nursery are not exclusionary. For example, the girls make two mother's day cards. Don't assume 'nuclear' families, etc. It will also be important that staff understand the nature of the 'foster parent' alongside any same-sex parent issues. Diversity in families is a growing fact, so staff awareness of this is important.*

Some practitioners expressed views about parents making 'choices' and how the system cannot always meet the needs which arise from life choices:

> Mother and toddler groups are a tradition. Mothers have rights to their group too. They don't always want men there. They talk about things that are important to women.

> Travelling families can't expect to get priority over the local community. ... Pandering to whims of people who choose to travel around could mean that people in the community lose out – can't have it all ways!

> If people come to this country they get free education and preschool provision. They can't really expect staff to speak foreign languages. I think they should just have to learn English. Perhaps that seems harsh but, well, that's what I think.

> I don't think sexuality is an issue so there's nothing really to consider on whether the parent is lesbian or not – it's a personal matter.

One member of the group lit something of a firework when, having discussed the above issues at length, she said:

> There are times when I think I'm the one who is excluded. I sometimes think that it really doesn't matter what I think or how I feel, I get the feeling that I'm just there to serve everyone else. Never mind supporting me, it's just do this, do that, never mind my opinion or my beliefs. So inclusion has to work both ways really. I think my views matter too. I want to feel included in my work setting. Then I'd find it less difficult to include the parents that make me feel, well, uncomfortable... yeah, uncomfortable.

Conclusion

From our research – reported throughout this book – we understand that the majority of early years practitioners are committed to developing inclusive communities of learning for the youngest children, where families feel valued and supported and are able to contribute to the development of the settings. What is clear, however, is that a small number of practitioners feel that they are rarely consulted. They feel at times that they are there simply to do the bidding of management and senior staff, and policy makers and parents, and not all practitioners feel that their professional knowledge, skills and attitudes are recognised. However, there are also inclusive settings where managers work hard to ensure that their staff (as well as the children and parents) feel a sense of ownership, citizenship and belonging and that they too feel – and indeed are – included.

Since I started here I've felt so, so at home. I've always been asked what I think about things, and when my ideas haven't been taken up I get an explanation as to why it won't work, ya know? I feel like, well, like I make a real contribution.
(Amy, Foundation Stage teacher in her second year of teaching)

Workshop 9 How inclusive are you?

Staff may wish to work on either or both of the activities in Boxes 9.2 or 9.3 to (i) place themselves on the inclusion/segregation continuum and (ii) identify inclusion/exclusion issues in relation to a range of situations. These activities can be used to identify further needs in terms of professional development and/or changes in practice and policy within the setting.

Policy points

The Equality Act 2010

Section 85 (p. 55) states that:

'(2) The responsible body of a school to which this section applies must not discriminate against a pupil:

a in the way it provides education for the pupil;
b in the way it affords the pupil access to a benefit, facility or service;
c by not providing education for the pupil;
d by not affording the pupil access to a benefit, facility or service;
e by excluding the pupil from the school;
f by subjecting the pupil to any other detriment.' (The National Archives, 2010, s. 85, p. 55)

The Equality Act 2010 states that a school must not discriminate against a pupil in the way it provides education. To discriminate is to distinguish and separate, which disputes Nutbrown's (2002b, p. 2) acknowledgement of the 'philosophy, pedagogy and purpose' of early years tradition. Implicit within key curriculum documents is an approach to practice with young children which seeks to be attuned, responsive, relational, collaborative and inclusive and is articulated throughout.

The strength of the curriculum documents, of course, is the extent to which they move from rhetoric to reality. Pupils are not the only souls in danger of discrimination if the ethos which underpins the documentation is not an understood, lived actuality. The question is not are all children, are all parents, are all staff embraced with equal esteem as they connect in different ways with different settings, but do all children, do all parents, do all staff feel a sense of worth and belonging?

1 'A duty to make reasonable adjustments applies to the responsible body of such a school:
2 In relation to England and Wales, this section applies to:

   a   a school maintained by a local authority;
   b   an independent educational institution (other than a special school);
   c   a special school (not maintained by a local authority). ...

3 In relation to Scotland, this section applies to:

   a   a school managed by an education authority;
   b   an independent school;
   c   a school in respect of which the managers are for the time being receiving grants under section 73(c) or (d) of the Education (Scotland) Act 1980.'

Further reading

Arnold, C. (2012) *Improving Your Reflective Practice through Stories of Practitioner Research*. London: Routledge.

Booth, T., Ainscow, M., Black-Hawkins, K., Vaughan, M. and Shaw, L. (2006) *Index for Inclusion: Developing Learning and Participation and Play* (2nd edition). Bristol: Centre for Studies in Inclusive Education. The Index is available from: CSIE, 1 Redland Close, Elm Lane, Redland, Bristol BS6 6UE.

10

Including: the future

Introduction

As we noted at the beginning of this book, policy during the 1990s was in the main a matter of *prescription* which included:

- National Curriculum and subsequent revisions;
- inspection;
- Children Act 1989;
- Codes of practice for the identification of children with SEN;
- Baseline Assessment;
- targets for children and adults;
- new 'thresholds' for staff achievement and professional development;
- admission of 4 year olds in school;
- Early Years Child Care Partnerships – diversification;
- *National Literacy Strategy* (DfEE, 1998);
- *National Numeracy Strategy* (DfEE, 1999).

This list identifies but a few of the major policy developments which impacted on early years education during that time. Examination of policies affecting the early years have, it seems, moved from excessive *prescription* to what we might view as a form of *revolution*, in part, as a result of devolution of political power in some UK countries.

The prescription of curriculum, assessment, pedagogy of literacy and numeracy and codes of practice in relation to SEN had collectively narrowed curriculum and provision and, increasingly, many practitioners felt that early years provision was becoming less and less appropriate for many young children and militated especially against the inclusion of children who were, in some way, 'different' from many of their peers.

To summarise, the 1990s and early 2000s saw intensive policy intervention in the early years and then devolution brought new policy shift. In England, these were manifest in:

- Foundation Stage;
- Foundation Stage Profile;
- *Birth to Three Matters* (DfES, 2002);
- *Every Child Matters* – The Children Act 2004 (DfES, 2004).

The re-emergence of play in the curriculum through the Foundation Stage curriculum marked a recognition of the needs of children aged between 3 and 5 years, and the replacement of Baseline Assessment at age 4 with the formative 'Foundation Stage Profile'. This was designed to be compiled throughout the child's time in the Foundation Stage and was seen by some as a relief from the domination of targets, which some children (at 4 years) failed to achieve. And, as we have seen in Chapters 1 and 2, across the United Kingdom, Sure Start – a major policy development which impacted significantly on inclusive practices (Weinberger, Pickstone and Hannon, 2005) – brought with it not only major policy shifts but an unprecedentedly high level of resources.

Nationally and locally, in England, Northern Ireland, Scotland and Wales, Sure Start programmes have brought together existing initiatives and developed new projects to address a range of educational, medical, economic and social issues, including poverty, ill health, addictions – all the elements in communities and lives which create exclusion and ghetto-ise families and communities. It may even be safe to say that Sure Start in some areas of the UK has made strides in tackling social and educational exclusion.

So, in the context of rapid shifts in policy and a political agenda for change which acknowledged the importance of early intervention policies to address social exclusion, what does the future look like for inclusion in the early years and what developments are needed in order to realise inclusive early education and care? The studies which form the basis of this book point to several key factors which must be given priority if the future is to be inclusive. Throughout the book we have reflected the views of many early childhood educators from a range of settings and services in the UK on the inclusion of young children. The suggestions we make here draw on two studies, one involving UK practitioners, and a wider European study (Clough and Nutbrown, 2004; Nutbrown and Clough, 2004), part of which has been reported in Chapter 6. Our suggestions also connect with research studies identified in the earlier part of this book. What does the future look like for inclusion in the early years? We suggest that there are four central concerns that must be addressed: professional development for practitioners; a shared dialogue; citizenship for young children; resources and policy commitment.

Professional development for practitioners

In Chapter 6 we demonstrated how professional development opportunities for preschool educators were a key issue for the practitioners in our study, and a small number said that their professional development was of a high level:

> *I did an MEd and specialised in SEN and young children. Fantastic, I learned so much and became my own 'expert'. I still read so much, particularly around managing behaviour and particular EBD issues.* (Nursery teacher in Scotland)

It appears that those who valued their professional development particularly highly were experienced professionals who had studied at postgraduate level, gaining academic awards for their efforts. For some, however, professional development opportunities for inclusion were minimal or even non-existent:

> *I've had no professional development really. Occasional training but not always when required.* (Preschool leader in Aberdeenshire)

> *I've had Autism Awareness training, however, I don't feel qualified or really informed enough to give the support children with SEN deserve.* (Nursery teacher in Wales)

However, most said that they learned most about including young children who were somehow 'different' or had specific difficulties from working with knowledgeable others who were willing to share their experiences.

In the following extract in Box 10.1 from her own autobiography, Mary reflects on aspects of her own professional development which were derived from working with and alongside a headteacher who inspired and supported her *thinking* as well as her actions. We can begin to understand something of Mary's beliefs about children and childhood and teaching from the following extracts, which tell something of the early influences on her beliefs and values. In Mary's own words:

Box 10.1 'Mary McVeigh'

It was [here] at my first school, an ordinary junior school, it could be said, but with an extraordinary headteacher, where I began to learn about children learning. It was far removed from techniques of teaching, more in the cultivation of a personal philosophy which sought to characterise relationships with children in terms of respect and understanding. The empathy and rapport which defined the relationship this headteacher had with the children in his care has been profoundly influential throughout my teaching career and of primary importance when I meet new children whatever their age.

It was here I became aware of the value of dialogue. Not just as part of teaching but more importantly in the relationships we were encouraged to form with the children in our care. To take time to listen to children, to their concerns, their reasons for being or doing, to be accepting and compassionate was part of the strong ethos of the school.

I would be drawn back on several occasions to seek guidance and direction over the years in an unconscious acknowledgement of the significance of that early experience and the influence it had in terms of how I approach my work with young children.

On another occasion whilst working at a special school, a seemingly wonderful opportunity presented itself. A trip to Lapland to meet Father Christmas. I was filled with trepidation for I knew that one of the young children in my group, an autistic boy, would find it extremely difficult to cope with such a change in routine. Encouraged by arrangements to intervene if this proved to be the case, off we set.

Not long after arriving at the airport the child became very upset and lay on the floor in the middle of the departure lounge shouting repeatedly 'This boy doesn't like crowds', surrounded by a curious public backing away. The experience again confirmed to me the imperative of understanding and respect when working with young children. It illustrates the dilemma of different agendas. The adult agenda compared with that of the child. An extreme example from a child with severe and complex learning needs but a stark reminder that we as practitioners should not ride roughshod, as it were, over the interests and concerns of the child, however altruistic the motive, in a selfish pursuit of what we think is right or, seen in a broader sense, what we think should be 'taught'.

I never felt anxious working in an environment with children who could react with extremes of behaviour. Pinching, biting and drawing blood, throwing objects, self-harm, smearing and screaming were part of many days. These were not interpreted as negative experiences but seen as opportunities to seek solutions, to change approach, to be reflective and evaluative in terms of practice. This aspect of my work with young children, so sharply brought into focus during my time at this special school, this special place, is something I endeavour to uphold in all my work with young children.

I had the opportunity to work with a visionary headteacher whose nursery practice is steeped in sound theory of how young children learn. It was here I experienced the joy of working with young children in a physical environment characterised by appropriateness, challenge and meaning, but more crucially, where I came to really explore play, its significance as a learning medium and my critical role within it.

(Continued)

(Continued)

I was able to immerse myself in the play experiences of young children yet soon recognised how easily the unrestrained adult can disturb the thinking patterns of young children with inappropriate, ill-timed, unfocused, intrusions designed to be supportive yet resulting in dilution of learning. The opportunity for deep learning is easily missed if adults working with young children are unable to interpret what children are doing in their play and are unaware of how and where to take them on.

Mary's movingly vivid and reflective account demonstrates how inclusion is not simply another word in the politically correct jargon. Inclusion is a deeply political response – a moral response – to the movement for social justice.

A shared dialogue

The early years practitioners who participated in our research held strong views on inclusion of children with learning difficulties and were willing to share these views with openness and honesty. As the chapters in this book have demonstrated, they variously 'make' the policies of the countries and learning communities in which they work into meaningful realities. To the fore in their thinking are the needs of *all* children, and their inclusive (or non-inclusive) practices are often developed and informed by their views of childhood and their beliefs about the roles of parents in the education of young children. The paper by Eve Cook and Cathy Nutbrown in Box 10.2 focuses on how isolation might be reduced for members of minority groups in societies when issues of war and conflict arise. It emphasises the importance promoting inclusive practices and eliminating discrimination through the development of a shared vocabulary and understanding by ensuring the sharing of information.

Box 10.2   Facing conflict: attitudes, strategies and responses

Introduction

Throughout history, war has been a reality in the lives of children somewhere in the world. Since the end of the Second World War, however, such difficult realities have been localised in the UK, confined to places where children come face to face with violence and horror: the **Troubles** in Northern Ireland, shootings at Dunblane, rioting in Oldham, the murders of two young girls in Soham. But to a large degree, it is fair to say that most young children in the UK are shielded from the horrors of war and violence which too many experience in other parts of the world.

For early years practitioners, the creation of a safe and nurturing environment is a priority. Armed conflict and acts of terrorism have no place in an early years setting. But, in early 2003, many practitioners faced the question of how to help young children deal with the overwhelmingly powerful images of war and conflict that were entering their homes daily on television. Young children were being exposed to pictures and descriptions of bombing and killing on a scale never before witnessed. Many adults found the 'embedded' journalism which brought the war into their homes a difficult experience to deal with. What impact might these images have had on children? And how might early years practitioners incorporate children's questions, worries (and excitement) around what they saw into their pedagogy of conflict resolution, care and nurture?

Personal values and emotional skills

Current policy in the UK promotes early years provision which helps children learn to be respectful and considerate of other people's feelings, with an emphasis on children's personal, social and emotional development. Curriculum guidances in each of the UK countries fundamentally agree on the skills which are important in this area, stating that young children under five should:

- understand what is right, what is wrong and why (QCA/DfEE, 2000)
- feel confident and be able to form relationships with other children and with adults (ACCAC, 1997)
- understand that people have different needs, views, cultures and beliefs that need to be treated with respect (QCA/DfEE, 2000)
- care for the environment and for other people in the community (Scottish Consultative Council on the Curriculum, 1999)
- understand how to respond appropriately in conflict situations (CCEA, 2003).

Working towards these goals demands much of the early years practitioners who work with young children. In fact, to do such difficult work and effectively support young children in this area of their learning and development, practitioners need to consider their own selves, their perspectives, their values and the beliefs which drive their practices. Such work is among the most difficult that early years educators must do.

Values and moral positions are conveyed by every action in every setting. Adults must think about their own values and beliefs and what the shared vision in their setting might be (Nutbrown, 1996). Educators need also to have a sense of their own value so that they can truly value others. This can

(Continued)

(Continued)

be difficult in the early years, when many staff may feel undervalued, some working for low pay and often in difficult conditions. Under such circumstances educators can feel quite powerless – yet they *are* powerful, and critically so in terms of the impact they have on young children's decision-making, and in shaping the ideas and beliefs of young minds, souls and spirits (Nutbrown and Drummond, 1996). In the early years, children are developing moral concepts and values in their homes, settings, local communities and the wider world, and they need adults who are mature in their own thinking around difficult issues, who can support them in this most important aspect of their learning and development.

Parents and practitioners want to enable children to grow up with an understanding of the social norms of their culture and the social conventions determined by it, but also to be able to grasp the moral issues of fairness, human welfare and justice. Early years practitioners aim to encourage such moral characteristics as empathy, compassion and kindness, and recognise the importance of self-esteem in that process (Dyer, 2002). These are huge tasks within which some complex issues are embedded.

Crucially, in this area of work, early years pedagogy means more than the work practitioners do – it means thinking about and reflecting upon practice, principles and theories and the creation of a working framework which is shared (in meaningful ways) by all concerned, in the context of personal, cultural and community values (Singer and Hännikainen, 2002).

Adults in early years settings are very powerful people, and their power relationships between themselves and children may need to be reframed so that the moral intent is clear and children are supported in their own moral decision-making.

Playing out violent scenes

After the attack on the Twin Towers in New York on 11 September 2001, many early years settings reported that children were building and demolishing towers. Of course, young children have always used bricks to do that – but what was worrying was the context of images which fuelled these actions. During the Iraq War in early 2003, where 24-hour television reported the unfolding of the war minute by minute, many children were seen playing 'battles' with toy figures. So how should adults respond to such play?

Adult responses to all children's play is fuelled by strong personal beliefs, and nowhere is this more evident than in responses to play stimulated by images of war and terror. 'Guns and weapons play give rise to strong emotions in early years settings. Teams often have deeply held reservations about aggressive forms of play and socio-dramatic themes' (Lindon, 2001).

With television film of military personnel carrying guns and footage showing graphic images of destruction and violence at a time when children are watching, it is inevitable that some young children will play out what they see. Holland (1999) argues that practitioners are concerned that gun and weapon play will lead to more aggressive behaviour, creating problems in the management of children in the setting. Yet, according to her, when one setting removed its ban on war and weapon play, that aspect of their play became richer because it no longer had to be 'secret' and adults could support its development so that it was extended by the children into their drawing and mark-making.

Others have argued that war play promotes militaristic values and gives children (boys in particular) the message that hurting, killing and threatening others is acceptable. Walters' study of the perspectives of parents working in the armed forces on children's toys reports the importance (for adults) of the boundaries between what is 'real' and what is 'pretend'. Walters writes:

> One parent said that guns should not be seen as a plaything. 'Every time we go in or out of camp you see the soldiers on the gate with guns. That's where they should stay. I tell my children that they are for Daddy's work, to help him stop any bad people, they are not to play with.' (Walters, 2002: 130)

Miedzian (1992) suggested that 'violence toys' ultimately play a large part in socialising young boys into a culture of violence where war and violence are acceptable. Such a stance may be founded in the belief that children are unable to separate out reality and fantasy, but it is often the adults who confuse the two, taking literally what is intended by children as part of their make-believe. Many practitioners and parents will recall examples where they have over-played and are told by a child: 'It's not real, it's only pretend.' But herein lie some difficult questions.

- Can children really tell the difference between 'real' war and 'pretend' war if they see both forms in the media?
- Is 'war-play' different from 'home corner play' or 'hospital play'?
- Can practitioners make war play more 'healthy' if they get involved themselves? And how should they do that?

These are difficult questions, which practitioners need to ponder in order to uncover their own personal-professional positions and work out their own responses to these issues when children choose to confront them in early years settings.

Some difficulties may arise if parents do not understand – or disagree with – the approach the setting chooses to take around working through these issues with children. Some may feel that children should be shielded from such troubling things, not confronted with them. But as with all aspects of setting policy, regular and open dialogue with parents can help parents and staff find solutions to such difficult problems, perhaps through involving parents in the development of a strategy on the issue.

(Continued)

(Continued)

Working with children's emotions

Before using any strategy to support children's emotions, it is vital that practitioners and children have a shared 'language of emotions'. Practitioners need to be able to speak to each other in terms they share and understand and they also need to help children develop a vocabulary for saying how they feel and expressing a range of emotions. Practitioners may need to enrich their own vocabulary in order to talk through troubling issues and work with children on developing the rich vocabulary they need to describe their feelings and questions. The development of such a language will enhance the effectiveness of the strategies described below. While there are many more ways of working to support children's emotions, the strategies given here have been very successful over time.

Listening and talking

Children may try to make sense of overwhelming feelings through their play – they may change the ending of distressing events or alter the power balance by putting themselves in charge of situations where they felt helpless. Playing out disturbing episodes or scenes does not mean that children will find solutions to their worries nor is it always possible for adults to know what the intentions are behind a child's play. However, a respectful educator can skilfully judge how to help children come to some resolution with difficult issues.

In Reggio Emilia the staff, children and parents explored their feelings about the war in Kosovo together. Later, the children's words about war and peace were produced on large white banners which were 'grandly and publicly displayed' in the town (Abbott and Nutbrown, 2001: 48). The positioning of the banners and the respect shown for the words of the children reflects how children are viewed in Reggio – as valuable members of the community with important and valuable contributions to make. The Reggio educators had the courage to put children's thoughts centre stage and to confront children's learning about war and conflict in a spirit of learning 'in community'. It is this willingness to talk and think with children, to respect their perspectives and ideas that should be central to working with young children.

During the Iraq War, many children witnessed graphic television accounts of destruction, injury and death – and it is possible that the impact on children living in homes where the television is a constant accompaniment to daily life could have been profound. This is what four-year-old Alice said to an adult in her playgroup during the war: 'The bomb aeroplane is going to come over from Baghdad and it's going to drop a bomb on playgroup and then on the village. All the soldiers are going to get killed, that's for sure. Don't drop on our house 'cos we're not going to be pleased, only drop it on bad people.'

Alice had clearly absorbed a great deal of information, and in these comments expresses her fears for the safety of her village, her playgroup and her home. She was working out what the reason might be for dropping bombs, and had arrived at the conclusion that it must be because the people are 'bad'. Children may also be absorbing the message that these 'bad' people are different from them – that they are black or Muslim or from another country or speaking a different language. Children notice racial differences at a young age and begin to attribute values to those differences (Milner, 1983). Practitioners need to be informed about how children can learn racist attitudes and the issues which arise from this so that they can help children to challenge these ideas.

A bomb probably will not drop on Alice in her remote village in a largely rural county in England, but a bomb did drop on Ali in Baghdad. Bombs have exploded in other parts of the UK, and many other children and their families around the world have been affected by war and violence. Adults working with young children have a responsibility to understand and address the differing impact and experience of war for all children. Although Ali was flown to better hospital treatment amid a flurry of media coverage, many thousands of children were not and they still suffer. Meanwhile, some young children in early childhood education settings in the UK still play 'war' and 'bombing'.

Persona dolls

If children are to manage these complex emotions, they will need to explore and discuss them in a context that makes sense to them. Persona dolls provide an opportunity for practitioners to work on a wide range of issues which require moral reasoning in a way that is meaningful and appropriate to young children (Brown, 2001). Practitioners in the setting create a persona for the doll they will introduce to the children; together they decide the doll's heritage, where he/she lives and with whom. They think about simple things like what food the doll likes, what games they enjoy and what their favourite TV programme might be. The doll is the practitioner's doll and is not simply a toy for children to use. At the first visit the doll will sit on the practitioner's lap and just be introduced sharing information about themselves. At a later stage the doll may ask for the children's help in solving a problem, for example: Sue would not let some children play in the home corner because 'you are a boy and only girls play here', or why Bob said they had to be the patient not the doctor 'because you have a hearing aid'. In a setting recently, one doll, Baljit, told the children how upset he was when someone called him a nasty name and said he should go home to his own country. The children were asked by the practitioner what they would have done if they had been there and they offered their suggestions, 'I would have held his hand', 'I would have played with him'. They considered the name calling – how do they feel if

(Continued)

(Continued)

someone calls them a name? They were asked to consider what Baljit felt and finally to offer some suggestions about what he could do now: 'Tell his mum', 'Tell the teacher to talk to the children', and from one child 'Make a rule about calling names'.

Over time, using the dolls, the children have the opportunity to learn about diverse cultures and beliefs, to consider other perspectives and to think about their own role in solutions to problems. Use of persona dolls encourages children to think jointly about solutions which are meaningful to them. They encourage the kind of solutions which reflect both care for others and a sense of justice, and also promote discussion about social conventions. However, as Farmer (2002) points out, it is critical that adults explore their own attitudes before they work with children in this way. Adults in any setting will need to work as a team to create a persona for the doll they decide to use, and this may involve everyone talking openly about the stereotypes they hold for differing groups of people. It may also prompt them to think about what they know and don't know about the circumstances of particular groups of people. What, for example, might the persona of a doll who was an asylum seeker look like? And before working with persona dolls, practitioners must carefully examine their practices, repressive rules, body language, personal knowledge and responses to children's questions, comments and play.

Children talking together

Circle time – whether or not it is called that – has become an established part of the session in many early years settings (Mosely, 2001).

A group size of around ten children would seem to be the best way to ensure that everyone has a chance to be heard in the time available (usually ten minutes). Circle time provides an opportunity for listening to the children and encouraging them to listen and take turns with one another. This is a complex and demanding skill – many adults cannot manage to wait their turn to speak.

The circle can provide a safe and friendly environment for children, even very quiet or shy children, to address problems and other issues. It can be used to discuss conflict situations that have arisen in the setting or beyond, or to discuss concerns expressed by children at other times without, of course, identifying the source. Circle time, like persona dolls, creates opportunities for children to think about their emotions and their relationships, rights and responsibilities towards others. The children are more motivated to join in discussions when the subject relates to their own lives and the situations they face during play in the nursery or in their daily lives.

Telling stories

Stories can also help children to think about moral dilemmas and give them the opportunity, will and desire to participate in thinking about solutions.

Persona dolls work well because they involve children in the stories that the dolls tell. There is, however, a rich heritage of stories both traditional and modern that invite children to think about moral issues. After a story about the Boy who cried Wolf, one five year old was outraged that the adults had not come to save the boy. It is their job, he said, 'Adults have to look after the little kids'.

These stories provide start points for discussions and glimpses into other worlds and experiences. A wealth of issues can be discussed in these sessions – fairness, friendship, tolerance, love, selfishness and exclusion – and early engagement with them provides the building blocks with which children develop their moral perspectives. Dyer's (2002) work on developing emotional intelligence in nursery-age children considers these issues and makes the point that her work also afforded staff and parents the opportunity to grow. Stories are powerful means of opening up the world and of helping children 'story' parts of their own lives. They can have a positive effect, too, on children thinking and behaviour, as Gussin Paley reported:

> Frightened children can be calmed, the timid dare to emerge from hiding, and those too worried to speak and play can learn to tell their own stories and to listen to mine. (Gussin Paley, 1996)

Values for the future

In trying to make sense of how to deal with war and violence in the context of young children's learning, it is important to consider the whole purpose of education. What is it for and what are its *big* aims?

Does the **education** offered to young children in the UK give them the skills and attitudes they need to take their place as citizens of the world, with all the human understanding and uncertainty that role requires? Education is more than the mere acquisition of facts and knowledge. It is about using that information in order to work with others, to hear differing viewpoints and to have the courage, confidence and morality to challenge cruelty and injustice.

Adults, just like children, are social beings who accelerate their learning, thinking and understanding when they work in partnership. A common purpose will help equip early childhood educators to support young children's learning as they begin to understand that 'peace is not merely the absence of war' (Jawaharlal Nehru).

(*Source*: A version of this paper was first published in
Early Education, September 2003)

The preschool educators in our studies were broadly supportive of inclusive early education. As we have seen, few professionals in this study argued against inclusive practices, though many attached caveats to their pro-inclusive stance (what, in Chapter 6, we have called the 'yes – but...'

factor) that related to support, professional development and the desire to balance the needs of all children. Such as:

> Yes – but depending on the nature of their individual challenge and the ability of the teacher to support effectively that special need in her setting. (Steiner-Waldorf kindergarten teacher in England)

> Yes, in some cases, but not all. It must be beneficial to the SEN child but not disruptive to the other children. (Nursery nurse in Wales)

> It is hard, here, to truly include children who have no English. Occasionally we get one but we're not set up for that. And the mother can't help – she can't speak English either. (Preschool worker in Scotland)

Preschool educators' responses and emphases varied according to professional background and experience of systems and settings. Attention to the voices, for example, of Steiner-Waldorf kindergarten teachers, shows clear and particular values and beliefs about children in the context of a nurturing environment. It is striking, too, that a pro-inclusive stance was often to be found in the voices of educators from Northern Ireland, perhaps influenced by many years of working in a divided society.

Throughout this book we have reported the experiences of some practitioners who discussed, not without some pain, some difficult issues and talked honestly about their fears and personal prejudices. We were struck by the openness of participants and by their willingness to discuss some deeply complex issues. Somehow they found ways to talk together about these difficult things. Reflecting on the process, one participant in our study said:

> Hearing what other people felt made it possible for me to admit how I really felt about things. Sometimes, you're afraid to say... well, you're reluctant to admit that, well... that it's not easy to involve all parents – or include all children. It's important that people can talk about the difficult things and sometimes say difficult things because it is really... only if we can really admit how we feel that we can begin to address those bits of our thinking, well, that aren't 'right' – things that hold prejudice and make us discriminatory in our practices – even if we try not to be.

In our studies, practitioners seemed to want to address their expressed prejudices and all said that they felt they could only do so in 'safe' circumstances, where it was clearly understood that practitioners were sharing personal responses and experiences in the spirit of seeking to be more inclusive in their practices. In talking about situations where they felt they were not operating inclusively was seen, by the participants in our study, as a step towards addressing any exclusive tendencies they held.

Developing a shared dialogue is essential. Our study leads us to suggest that, though difficult, finding ways to talk together about sometimes nega-tive feelings and attitudes as well as to discuss their many successful prac-tices is an important element in developing a pro-inclusive ethos and realising the vision of an inclusive future to early years education and care.

Citizenship for young children

Young children must be acknowledged as citizens in the communities in which they live and learn. In Chapter 8, Robin Taylor explained how he used large-scale art to bring together the various members of his school community. His work was inspired by the practices of Reggio Emilia in Italy and the New Zealand early years curriculum framework *Te Whariki* (NZ Ministry of Education, 1995), both of which can support practition-ers as they seek to develop practices which promote the citizenship of young children from birth.

The notion of citizenship lies, we suggest, at the heart of the Reggio Emilia approach to education, which has been developed through genera-tions and evolved, originally, from a resolve to provide a better future from children following the years of occupation during the Second World War. The children who attend Reggio Emilia Centres benefit from the invest-ment and commitment of those who have gone before, who created the foundations of an approach to preschool pedagogy based on community and citizenship. Central to the Reggio approach are carefully articulated theories of children as powerful competent learners, as users of multiple forms of expression, of the need for educators to listen to children, and of the importance of the environment in facilitating children's learning. The whole environment is crucial in the Reggio system and, as Malaguzzi, founder of the Reggio approach to preschool education, wrote:

> ... we consider the environment to be an essential constituent element of any theoretical or political research in education. We hold to be equally valuable the rationality of the environment, its capacity for harmonious coexistence, and its highly important forms and functions. Moreover, we place enormous value on the role of the environment as a motivation and animating force in creating spaces for relations, options and emo-tional and cognitive situations that produce a sense of well-being and security.
>
> It has been said that the environment should act as a kind of aquarium, which reflects the ideas, ethics, attitudes and culture of the people who live in it. (Malaguzzi, 1996, p. 40)

Those preschool environments are distinctive in character, with their open central *piazza* where children meet and play and share, communal dining spaces where food is shared over leisurely conversation, mirrors and light spaces for exploring shape and space from different angles, the *atelier* (the art studio) where children work with the *atelierista* (the experienced and qualified artist on the staff). Colour and light are all important, as are documentary descriptions of the various projects children have carried out. The distinctiveness of the environments is difficult to describe but Leask's description of her son's infant-toddler centre gives a flavour:

> ... Entering the school for the first time, the impact of my first impressions of so many years before came flooding back as we looked around a light open space filled with examples of children's work (but this was August – why weren't the walls bare?), written panels illustrated with photos, plants, a mix of small chairs and antique furniture, *bric-a-brac*, tiny beautiful treasures, delicate old objects and instruments, photos and examples of work that had obviously been there for many years – the sort of domestic archaeology layering that takes place over time in all our homes. (Leask, 2001, pp. 43–4)

What comes through in Leask's description is one of 'belonging' – of being a citizen in an inclusive culture of living and learning. *Te Whariki* is the New Zealand Ministry of Education's early childhood curriculum policy statement (*Te Whàriki Màtauranga mò ngà Mokopuna o Aotearoa*). *Te Whariki* is a framework for providing for *tamariki*/children's early learning and development within a socio-cultural context. It emphasises the learning partnership between *kaiako*/teachers, parents, *whānau*/ families. *Kaiako*/teachers weave an holistic curriculum in response to *tamariki*/children's learning and development in the early childhood setting and the wider context of the child's world.[1]

Te Whariki is a bilingual document which sets out the curriculum policy and framework from birth to five in New Zealand. It has been widely acclaimed in many other countries and, similar to the inspirational work of Reggio Emilia, has inspired an interest in practices and policies in early childhood which see children as central to their community and see learning as a shared experience. For this reason, many early childhood educators have an interest in the *Te Whariki* framework and the principles which underpin it. The *Te Whariki* document opens with a Maori poem followed by these words:

> Early childhood is '... a period of momentous significance for all people growing up in [our] culture ... By the time this period is over, children will have formed conceptions of themselves as social beings, as thinkers, and as language users, and they will have reached certain important decisions about their own abilities and their own worth'. (Donaldson et al., 1983, p. 1)

---

[1] Education Review Office, www.ero.govt.nz/publications/*Te Whariki*.

The *Te Whariki* sets out the principles, strands and goals for the early childhood years, appropriately differentiated for babies, toddlers and young children. 'Curriculum' is defined as 'the sum total of the experiences, activities, and events, whether direct or indirect, which occur within an environment designed to foster children's learning and development' (p. 10).

There are four foundation *principles* for the early childhood curriculum:

1 *Empowerment – Whakamana*: the early childhood curriculum empowers the child to learn and grow;
2 *Holistic Development – Kotahitanga*: the early childhood curriculum reflects the holistic way children learn and grow;
3 *Family and Community – Whànau Tangata*: the wider world of family and community is an integral part of the early childhood curriculum;
4 *Relationships – Ngà Hononga*: children learn through responsive and reciprocal relationships with people, places and things. (Carr and May, 2000)

Carr and May (2000) describe how the development of the New Zealand early childhood curriculum rejected a subject-based framework and favoured instead 'strands': *well-being, belonging, contributing, communicating* and *exploring*. The strands and goals arise from the principles and are woven around these principles in patterns that reflect the diversity of each early childhood education service. Together, the principles, strands, goals and learning outcomes set the framework for the curriculum *whàriki* (*whariki* being the Maori word for 'mat'). The ethos behind *Te Whariki* is that every child has a curriculum mat fitting his/her needs, culture and personality. Everyone is different, but each has the same principles and strands in its warp and weft. Other strands, which are more individually defined, can be added to this, making curriculum for every child unique and appropriate.

Citizenship, then, for young children means creating a culture of belonging in their early years settings – where *all* contribute, *all* learn and *all* are valued.

The study of children's views of their early years settings reported in Chapter 7 was an illustration of the importance of consulting all members of a learning community and, importantly, of acting on them.

Citizenship and peace

The concept of using the media to promote peace with young children was developed by the Peace Initiatives Institute (Pii), Colorado, USA. The Media Initiatives For Children (MIFC) aims to:

teach young children the value of respecting – and including – others who are different from themselves.

MIFC uses mass media such as public television alongside a preschool/ school-based programme of activities and materials to change in the attitudes and behaviours of young children who live in and have experienced conflict. The aim is to influence young children's values in their early years, with the hope of having an impact on their beliefs, values and behaviours in adulthood. This, therefore, is a long-term initiative whose impact may not be visible for many years. In Belfast, Northern Ireland, the Peace Initiatives Institute and NIPPA (The Early Years Organisation) developed the first MIFC for Northern Ireland. Following a pilot, the programme began throughout Northern Ireland in 2005. Initially, in 200 schools (some 1,000 preschool age children and their practitioners, parents and siblings), the programme, evaluated by the National Foundation for Educational Research at Queen's University Belfast, was planned to extend throughout Northern Ireland, with future extensions into the Republic of Ireland.[2]

Initial responses of the children who experienced the pilot programme included such comments as:

> *You shouldn't leave anybody else out.*
> *The colour of a person's skin shouldn't stop you from playing with them.*
> *It's what is on the inside that is important.*
> *We have to learn to trust each other.*

As Cook and Nutbrown (in Box 10.2) point out, education for peace is an essential part of education for citizenship, creating communities where young children can live and learn together peacefully and respectfully, respecting and celebrating the differences which make them each unique.

Professional development

Initial and continuing professional development for all who work in home and group settings has been the focus of the Nutbrown Review of Early Education and Care qualifications. The Review (Nutbrown, 2012) noted the importance of training in issues relating to equality for all practitioners, whatever their level of qualification or job role.

---

[2]Further information is available from www.mifc-pii.org/ and www.qub.ac.uk/ research-centres/CentreforEffectiveEducation

Lane (2008) argued that:

> Early years services and settings should be safe places free from discrimination and harassment where everyone is treated with dignity, valued and given equal respect and concern. Policies, procedures, practices and any curriculum changes take time and thought. The important thing is to start the process. (p. 292)

Offering a framework for racial equality, Lane (2008) advocates that early years services and those working in settings, should identify the components that relate most to their settings, think about the points that need immediate attention, and consider how they might get help to address them. She states that:

> Training and education for racial equality in the early years is in its infancy with regard to its proven effectiveness. ... Short one-off sessions that do not address the underlying causes of inequality are very likely to be ineffective. (Lane, 2008, p. 150)

Lane makes the case for sustained professional development, provided by knowledgeable and skilled educators, is essential across all levels and types of courses for early years workers.

We have already discussed the usefulness of the *Index for Inclusion* (Booth et al., 2000) as a tool for whole setting professional development (see Chapter 9).

Resources and policy commitment

As we have seen, investment in Sure Start programmes of the early 2000s has brought about effective developments in provision for families – meeting differently expressed needs with wide-ranging services and reaching families and young children who might otherwise not access more traditional forms of early childhood education and care provision. The present plans to offer early years services to the 40% most vulnerable 2 year olds by 2015 is another indicator of the investment in early years services as a preventative measure, a way of inhibiting difficulty and enhancing learning and life changes later.[3] There can be no doubt that properly funded policy commitments are an essential ingredient to inclusive futures in Early Childhood Education and Care.

---

[3]http://www.education.gov.uk/childrenandyoungpeople/earlylearningandchildcare/
delivery/free%20entitlement%20to%20early%20education/b0070114/
eefortwoyearolds.

Conclusion

Finally, the various narratives throughout this book show that there is much good practice to include parents, families, staff and communities in the provision and development of early years education and care. At the same time there remains much to learn about the ways in which various policies of UK countries are realised in practice and how practitioners' views are embodied in their setting-based work. Professional development for all early childhood practitioners is essential if they are to continue to learn how to include all children and their families, to create a climate of cooperative citizenship and to provide quality experience for young children through equality policies and practices. A task for future research includes the ways in which practitioners learn to embrace difference and diversity and tackle exclusion, and promote inclusion, from a position of knowledge and moral commitment to fairness and social justice. We hope that this book will further support research and practice to promote truly inclusive early years provision where *all* belong and where exclusion is an action from a past era. We hope that the personal experiences reported in this book will support researchers, practitioners and policy makers in reaching the point where *inclusion* is not simply a word, or an idea, but a political, social, economic, educational and human reality for *all* young children, their families and communities.

Workshop 10 Including: the future

Our research and review of current research and practices leads us to conclude that four issues must be addressed in order to further the broad inclusion agenda:

- Professional development for practitioners;
- A shared dialogue;
- Citizenship for young children;
- Resources and policy commitment.

Staff may wish to consider their perspectives on these four issues as discussed in this chapter. They may also want to add issues of their own which they feel important if their settings are to move forward inclusively. This may be a point at which to discuss outcomes of earlier workshop discussions.

Policy points

The Equality Act 2010 (The National Archives, 2010, p. 55) states that a responsible body 'must not victimise a person or pupil' and refers to occasions where false evidence may be given, allegations made, or actions carried out in bad faith. Although the parameters of these references are made explicit in the Act, there is an unsaid inference here, one of fractured or deficient relationships.

Brooker (2011, p. 140) understood the place of relationships within learning environments, and those which may be at the threshold of these environments, in questioning whether there is a determination by practitioners to take serious account of the perspectives of others. Her context was children and hearing their views but, arguably, there is a wider implication here about recognition and acceptance. This is a concern for all those who can, and must, be enabled to take their place in a shared dialogue of mutual importance.

Sandberg and Heden (2011, p. 328) discussed the consequence of perception in highlighting the significance of how actions are perceived and meaning understood.

Through encouragement or censure, particular perspectives are revealed and 'messages are conveyed'. There is a concealed implication here and a deeper, more significant anxiety if this is realised within the context of relationships in settings. When the message practitioners convey is one of openness, sincerity and acceptance, with an expectation that partnerships are collective, the disquiet described within the Equality Act 2010 may be averted.

Important matters for the parent or practitioner must be able to be brought forward, when they are felt, and received with compassion for, as Rogoff (1990, p. 140) recognised, 'the model of most effective social interaction is to "attempt to understand", to consider alternative views'. That this applies to relationships between children and the adults who are most important to them should not be in question; that it should be a characteristic of the relationship between practitioners and parents is an obligatory ambition, if not already an existing welcome characteristic.

In the same spirit of receptiveness and flexibility, the Equality Act 2010 specifies that the responsible body of a school (or setting) 'must not victimise a person in the way it provides education for the pupil and in the way it affords the pupil access to a benefit, facility or service'. Seen in an egalitarian light, the affordance of professional development opportunities for staff within schools and settings is a vital and necessary consideration. Continuing opportunities to secure existing expertise and develop new skills and qualities, which enhance personal and professional practice, is an avenue along which those working within schools and settings should be able to progress. In addition, services offered at settings which support parents in their unique role as first educators of their child are vital prospects to be highlighted.

To return to the Equality Act 2010 and hear the sensitive language of victim, it is about feeling thwarted, disillusioned, disenchanted, even wounded. Unquestionably, however, an *including future* must be about celebrating the uniqueness of all the young souls for whom we are responsible, with the place of responsive interactions and receptive relationships being a necessary condition of practice.

Further reading

Brooker, L. (2011) Taking children seriously: an alternative agenda for research? *Journal of Early Childhood Research*, 9: 137.

The Home Office (2010) *Equality Act 2010*. London: HMSO.

Lane, J. (2008) *Young Children and Racial Justice: Taking Action for Racial Equality in the Early Years – Understanding the Past, Thinking about the Present, Planning for the Future*. London: National Children's Bureau.

Rogoff, B. (1990) *Apprenticeship in Thinking: Cognitive Development in Social Context*. Oxford: Oxford University Press.

Sandberg, A. and Heden, R. (2011) Play's importance in school. *Education*, 3(13): 317–29.

References

Abbott, L. and Nutbrown, C. (2001) *Experiencing Reggio Emilia*. Buckingham: Open University Press.

ACCAC (1997) *Desirable Outcomes for Children's Learning before Compulsory School Age*. Cardiff: Qualifications, Curriculum and Assessment Authority for Wales.

Ainscow, M., Booth, T. and Dyson, D. (2004) Understanding and Developing Inclusive Practices in Schools: A Collaborative Action Research Network. *International Journal of Inclusive Education*, 8(2): 125–139.

AGDEEW (2009) The Early Years Learning Framework in Australia, 'Being, Belonging and Becoming'. Australia.

Alderson, P. (2000) *Young Children's Rights: Exploring Beliefs, Principles and Practices*. London: Jessica Kingsley.

Allen, G. (2011) *Early Intervention: The Next Steps An Independent Report to Her Majesty's Government, Graham Allen MP*. Available at http://www.dwp.gov.uk/docs/early-intervention-next-steps.pdf

Alliance for Childhood (2004) *Tech Tonic: Towards a New Literacy of Technology*. College Park, MD: Alliance for Childhood. Available from: PO Box 444, College Park, MD 2074, USA; www.allianceforchildhood.org.

Amtsrådsforeningen (1998) *Statistik 1998*. Copenhagen: Amtsrådsforeningen.

Anderson, M. (1980) *Approaches to the History of the Western Family, 1500–1914*. London: Macmillan.

Angelides, P. (2000) A New Technique for Dealing with Behaviour Difficulties in Cyprus: The Analysis of Critical Incidents. *European Journal of Special Needs Education*, 15(1): 55–68.

Anning, A. and Ring, K. (2004) *Children's Drawings*. Buckingham: OUP.

Arnold, C. (2001) 'Persistence pays off: working with "hard to reach" parents'. In M. Whalley (ed.) and the Pen Green Centre Team, *Involving Parents in Their Children's Learning*. London: Paul Chapman Publishing.

Arnold, C. (2012) *Improving Your Reflective Practice through Stories of Practitioner Research*. London: Routledge.

Athey, C. (1990) *Extending Thought in Young Children: A Parent–Teacher Partnership*. London: Paul Chapman Publishing.

Athey, C. (1997) *Extending Thought in Young Children: A Parent–Teacher Partnership, second edition*. London: Sage.

Athey, C. (2007) *Extending Thought in Young Children* (2nd edition). London: Paul Chapman Publishing.

Aubrey, C., David, T., Godfrey, R. and Thompson, I. (2000) *Early Childhood Educational Research: Issues in Methodology and Ethics*. London: Falmer Press.

Avramidis, E. and Norwich, B. (2002) Teachers' Attitudes Towards Integration/Inclusion: A Review of the Literature. *European Journal of Special Needs Education*, 17(2): 129–47.

Baker, E.T., Wang, M.C. and Walberg, H.J. (1995) The Effects of Inclusion on Learning. *Educational Leadership*, 52(4): 33–5.

Balaguer, I. (2004) Social Management and Participation: Heart or Head in the Childhood Schools in Reggio. *Children in Europe*, 6(3): 31–2.

Barry, B. (2002) Social exclusion, social isolation and the distribution of income. In J. Hills, J. LeGrand and D. Piachaud (eds), *Understanding Social Exclusion*. Oxford: OUP.

Baz, P., Begun, L., Chia, K., Mason, G., Nutbrown, C. and Wragg, L. (1997) Working bilingually with families. In C. Nutbrown and P. Hannon (eds), *Preparing for Early Literacy Work with Families: A Professional Development Manual*. Nottingham/Sheffield: NES Arnold/REAL Project.

BERA (British Educational Research Association) (1977) *Early Years: Pedagogy, Curriculum and Adult Roles*. BERA: EYSIG.

Berry, T. (2001) Does inclusion work? A case study of four children. Unpublished MA in Early Childhood Education dissertation, University of Sheffield, Sheffield.

Berthelsen, D. and Brownlee, J. (2005) Respecting Children's Agency for Learning and Rights to Participation. *International Journal of Early Childhood*, 37(3): 49–60.

Booth, T. (2000) Reflection: Tony Booth. In P. Clough and J. Corbett, *Theories of Inclusive Education*. London: Sage.

Booth, T. and Ainscow, M. (2004) *Index for Inclusion: Developing Learning, Participation and Play in Early Years and Child Care*. Bristol: Centre for Studies in Inclusive Education.

Booth, T., Ainscow, M., Black-Hawkins, K., Vaughan, M. and Shaw, L. (2000) *Index for Inclusion: Developing Learning and Participation in Schools*. Bristol: Centre for Studies in Inclusive Education. Available from: CSIE, 1 Redland Close, Elm Lane, Redland, Bristol BS6 6UE.

Booth, T., Ainscow, M., Black-Hawkins, K., Vaughan, M. and Shaw, L. (2002) *Index for Inclusion: Developing Learning and Participation in Schools* (2nd edition). Bristol: Centre for Studies in Inclusive Education. Available from: CSIE, 1 Redland Close, Elm Lane, Redland, Bristol BS6 6UE.

Booth, T., Ainscow, M. and Kingston, D. (2006) *Index for Inclusion: Developing Play, Learning and Participation in Early Years and Childcare* (2nd edition). Bristol: Centre for Studies in Inclusive Education. The Index is available from: CSIE 1, Redland Close, Elm Lane, Redland, Bristol BS6 6UE.

Boyden, J. (1997) Childhood and policy makers: a comparative perspective on the globalisation of childhood. In A. James and A. Prout (eds), *Constructing and Reconstructing Childhood: Contemporary Issues in the Sociological Study of Childhood* (2nd edition). London: Routledge Falmer.

Bragg, S. (2007) 'But I Listen to Children Anyway': Teacher Perspectives on Pupil Voice. *Educational Action Research*, 15(4): 505–518.

Bredekamp, S. and Copple, C. (eds) (1997) *Developmentally Appropriate Practice in Early Childhood Programs* (revised edition). Washington, DC: National Association for the Education of Young Children.

Brooker, L. (2011) Taking Children Seriously: An Alternative Agenda for Research? *Journal of Early Childhood Research*, 9: 137.

Brown, B. (2001) *Combating Discrimination: Persona Dolls in Action*. Stoke-on-Trent: Trentham Books.

Bureau 2000/PMF_FOLA (1997) *Stistick om Danske Børns Institutionsliv 1996*. Copenhagen: Bureau 2000/PMF_FOLA.

Burnett., C and Myers, J. (2002) 'Beyond the Frame': Exploring Children's Literacy Practices. *Reading*, 36(2): 55–62, DOI: 10.1111/1467-9345.00187

Carr, M. and May, H. (1992) *Te Whariki* (Early Childhood Curriculum Development Project Final Report to the Ministry of Education). Hamilton, New Zealand: University of Waikato.

Carr, M. and May, H. (2000) Te Whariki: curriculum voices. In H. Penn (ed.), *Early Childhood Services: Theory, Policy and Practice* (pp. 55–73). Buckingham: Open University Press.

Carter, C. (2005) 'Developing Friendships in the Early Years: Playground Buddies.' Unpublished Masters dissertation, University of Sheffield.

Clay, M.M. (1975) *What Did I Write?* Auckland: Heinemann Educational.

Cook–Sather, A. (2002) *Authorizing Students' Perspectives: Toward Trust, Dialogue, and Change in Education* DOI: 10.3102/0013189X031004003

CCEA (2003) *The Revised Northern Ireland Primary Curriculum: Foundation Stage.* Belfast: Council for the Curriculum, Examinations and Assessment.

CCEA (2006) *Curriculum Understanding: The Foundation Stage (Northern Ireland).* Belfast: Council for the Curriculum, Examinations and Assessment.

CCEA (2007) *The Northern Ireland Curriculum Primary.* Belfast: Council for the Curriculum, Examinations and Assessment.

Centre for Studies in Inclusive Education (CSIE) (1995) *International Perspectives on Inclusion.* Bristol: CSIE.

Christensen, P. and James, A. (2000) *Research with Children: Perspectives and Practices.* London: Falmer Press.

Christmas, J. (2005) Is it OK to play? In K. Horst and C. Nutbrown (eds), *Perspectives on Early Education: Essays in Contemporary Research.* Stoke-on-Trent: Trentham Books.

Clark, A. and Moss, P. (2003) *The Mosaic Approach.* London: OUP.

Clark, A., McQuail, S. and Moss, P. (2003) *Exploring the Field of Listening to and Consulting with Young Children.* DFES: Nottingham.

Clay, M. (1972) *Stones: The Concepts about Print Test.* London: Heinemann.

Clough, P. (ed.) (1998) *Managing Inclusive Education: From Policy to Experience.* London: Paul Chapman Publishers/Sage.

Clough, P. (1999) Exclusive Tendencies: Concepts, Consciousness and Curriculum in the Project of Inclusion. *International Journal of Inclusive Education*, 3(1): 63–73.

Clough, P. (2000) Routes to inclusion. In P. Clough and J. Corbett, *Theories of Inclusive Education.* London: Paul Chapman Publishers.

Clough, D. and Clough, P. (forthcoming 2013) *Inclusion: A Communitarian Account.* (unpublished paper in press)

Clough, P. and Corbett, J. (2000) *Theories of Inclusive Education.* London: Paul Chapman Publishers/Sage.

Clough, P., Garner, P., Pardeck, J.T. and Yuen, F. (eds) (2004) *Handbook of Social and Emotional Difficulties.* London: Sage.

Clough, P. and Nutbrown, C. (2002) The Index for Inclusion: Personal Perspectives from Early Years Educators. *Early Education*, 36: 1–4.

Clough, P. and Nutbrown, C. (2003) The 'Index for Inclusion': perspectives of early years practitioners. In M. Nind, K. Sheehy and K. Simmons (eds), *Inclusive Education: Learners and Learning Contexts.* London: David Fulton.

Clough, P. and Nutbrown, C. (2004) Special Educational Needs and Inclusive Early Education: Multiple Perspectives from UK Educators. *Journal of Early Childhood Research*, 2(2): 191–211.

Coates, L. and Coates, A. (2006) Young Children Talking and Drawing. *International Journal of Early Years Education*, 14(3) 221–242.

Coles, R. (1997) *The Moral Intelligence of Children*. London: Bloomsbury.

Connolly, P. (2004) *Boys and Schooling in the Early Years*. London: Routledge Falmer.

Connolly, P., Smith, A. and Kelly, B. (2002) *Too Young to Notice? The Cultural and Political Awareness of 3–6 Year-olds in Northern Ireland*. Belfast: Northern Ireland Community Relations Council.

Cook-Sather, A. (2002) Authorizing Students' Perspectives: Towards Trust, Dialogue and Change in Education. *Educational Researcher*, 31(4): 3–14.

Copeland, I. (2000) Special Educational Needs in Primary and Secondary School Brochures in England. *European Journal of Special Needs Education*, 15(3): 241–54.

Cornoldi, C., Terreni, A., Scruggs, T. and Mastropieri, M. (1998) Teacher Attitudes in Italy after Twenty Years of Inclusion. *Remedial and Special Education*, 19(6): 350–6.

Critchley, D. (2002) Children's assessment of their own learning. In C. Nutbrown (ed.), *Research Studies in Early Childhood Education*. Stoke-on-Trent: Trentham Books.

Croll, P. and Moses, D. (2000) Ideologies and Utopias: Education Professionals' Views of Inclusion. *European Journal of Special Needs Education*, 15(1): 1–12.

Crowther, D., Dyson, A. and Millward, A. (2001) Supporting Pupils with Special Educational Needs: Issues and Dilemmas for Special Needs Coordinators in English Primary Schools. *European Journal of Special Needs Education*, 16(2): 85–97.

D'Arcy, S. (1990) Towards a non-sexist primary classroom. In E. Tutchell (ed.), *Dolls and Dungarees: Gender Issues in the Primary School Curriculum*. Milton Keynes: Open University Press.

Daniels, H., Visser, J., Cole, T. and de Reybekil, N. (1999) *Research Brief 90: Emotional and Behavioural Difficulties in Mainstream Schools*. London: Department for Education and Employment and the University of Birmingham.

Davie, R., Butler, N. and Goldstein, H. (1972) *From Birth to Seven: A Report of the National Child Development Study*. London: Longman/National Children's Bureau.

Davies, S. and Artaraz, K. (2009) Towards an Understanding of Factors Influencing Early Years Professionals' Practice of Consultation with Young Children. *Children and Society*, 23(1): 57–69.

Davies, B. (1989) *Frogs, Snails and Feminist Tales*. Sydney: George Allen & Unwin.

Department for Education (1994) *Code of Practice for the Identification and Assessment of SEN*. London: HMSO.

DENI (Department of Education in Northern Ireland) (1997) *Curricular Guidance*. Belfast: Department of Education, Northern Ireland.

DENI (Department of Education in Northern Ireland) (2004) *Review of Preschool Education in Northern Ireland*. Bangor, Co. Down: Department of Education.

Derman-Sparkes, L. and the ABC Task Force (1989) *Anti-Bias Curriculum: Tools for Empowering Young Children*. Washington, DC: National Association for the Education of Young Children.

DCSF (Department for Children, Schools and Families) (2004) *The Children Act 2004*. London: DCSF.

DCSF (Department for Children, Schools and Families) (2007) *The Early Years Foundation Stage.* London: DCSF.

DCSF (Department for Children, Schools and Families) (2008) *Early Years Foundation Stage Profile.* London: DCSF.

DCSF (Department for Children, Schools and Families) (2009) *Guide for Parents of Children with Special Educational Needs.* London: DCSF.

DES (Department of Education and Science) (1978) *The Warnock Report: Special Educational Needs: Report of the Committee of Enquiry into the Education of Handicapped Children and Young People.* London: Her Majesty's Stationery Office.

DES (Department of Education and Science) (1989a) *Starting with Quality – Report of the Rumbold Committee.* London: HMSO.

DES (Department of Education and Science) (1989b) *Education Under Five.* London: HMSO.

DES/DWP (2003) *Sure Start – An Introduction.* London: DfES/DWP.

DES (Department of Education and Science) (1988) *The Education Reform Act.* London: HMSO.

DES (Department of Education and Science) (1990) *Starting with Quality – Report of the Rumbold Committee.* London: HMSO.

DfE (Department for Education) (1988) *Education Reform Act.* London: Her Majesty's Stationery Office.

DfE (Department for Education) (1994) *Code of Practice for the Identification and Assessment of SEN.* London: Her Majesty's Stationery Office.

DfE (Department for Education) (2011) *Supporting Families in the Foundation Years.* London: Department for Education.

DfE (Department for Education) (2011) *The Tickell Review: The Early Years: Foundations for Life, Health and Learning.* London: DfE.

DfE (Department for Education) (2012) *Statutory Framework for the Early Years Foundation Stage: Setting the Standards for Learning, Development and Care for Children from Birth to Five.* London: Department for Education.

DfEE (Department for Education and Employment) (1996) *Desirable Outcomes of Nursery Education.* London: HMSO.

DfEE (Department for Education and Employment) (1997) *Excellence for All Children: Meeting Special Educational Needs.* London: HMSO.

DfEE (Department for Education and Employment) (1998) *National Literacy Strategy.* London: DfEE.

DfEE (Department for Education and Employment) (1999) *National Numeracy Strategy.* London: DfEE.

DfES (Department for Education and Skills) (1978) *The Education of Handicapped Children and Young People* (The Warnock Report). London: HMSO.

DfES (Department for Education and Skills) (1988) *The Education Reform Act.* London: HMSO.

DfES (Department for Education and Skills) (2002) *Birth to Three Matters: A Framework to Support Children in their Earliest Years.* London: DfES.

DfES (Department for Education and Skills) (2004) *The Children Act 2004.* London: HMSO.

The Home Office (2010) *Equality Act 2010.* London: HMSO.

Dewey, J. (1916) *Democracy and Education An introduction to the Philosophy of Education* New York: The Free Press.

Donaldson, M. (1983) *Children's Minds*. London: Penguin.

Draper, L. and Duffy, B. (2001) Working with parents. In G. Pugh (ed.), *Contemporary Issues in the Early Years: Working Collaboratively for Children*. London: Paul Chapman Publishing.

Dunn, J. (2004) *Children's Friendships: The Beginnings of Intimacy*. Oxford: Blackwell.

Dyer, P. (2002) A box full of feelings. In C. Nutbrown (ed.), *Research Studies in Early Childhood Education*. Stoke-on-Trent: Trentham Books.

Early Childhood Action (2012) 'Unhurried Pathways: A New Framework for Early Childhood: Accessed from: www.earlychildhoodaction.com (accessed February 2013)

Edwards, G., Gandini, L. and Forman, G. (eds) (2001) *The Hundred Languages of Children – The Reggio Emilia Approach to Early Childhood Education* (2nd edition). Norwood, NJ: Ablex.

Egelund, N. (2000) Country Briefing: Special Education in Denmark. *European Journal of Special Needs Education*, 15(1): 88–98.

Egelund, N. and Hansen, K.F. (2000) Behavioural Disorders in Danish Schools: A Qualitative Analysis of Background Factors. *European Journal of Special Needs Education*, 15(3): 285–96.

Eide, B. and Winger, N. (2005) From the Children's Point of View: Methodological and Ethical Challenges. In C. Clark, P. Moss and A.T. Kjørholt (eds), *Beyond Listening*. London: Routledge.

Elfer, P., Goldschmied, E. and Selleck, D. (2003) *Key Persons in the Nursery: Building Relationships for Quality Provision*. London: David Fulton.

Elfer, P. and Dearnley, K. (2007) Nurseries and Emotional Wellbeing. Evaluating an Emotionally Containing Model of Continuing Professional Development. *Early Years*, 27(3): 57–72.

Emanuelsson, I. (2001) Reactive versus Proactive Support Coordinator Roles: An International Comparison. *European Journal of Special Needs Education*, 16(2): 133–42.

European Convention on Human Rights (1994) *Convention for the Protection of Human Rights and Fundamental Freedoms*. Available at: www.echr.coe.int/NR/rdonlyres/D5CC24A7-DC13-4318-B457-5C9014916D7A/O/Convention_ENG.pdf

Farmer, G. (2002) Dolls with stories to tell. In C. Nutbrown (ed.), *Research Studies in Early Childhood Education*. Stoke-on-Trent: Trentham Books.

Field, F. (2012) *The Foundation Years: Preventing Poor Children Becoming Poor Adults: The Report of the Independent Review on Poverty and Life Chances*. London: HMSO. Available at: http://webarchive.nationalarchives.gov.uk/20110120090128/http:/povertyreview.independent.gov.uk/media/20254/poverty-report.pdf.

Firth, R. (1997) Brunswick Primary School 'Parents in Partnership' Project. In C. Nutbrown and P. Hannon (eds), *Preparing for Early Literacy Education with Parents: A Professional Development Manual*. Nottingham/Sheffield: NES Arnold/University of Sheffield School of Education.

Fletcher-Campbell, F. (2001) Issues of Inclusion: Evidence for Three Recent Research Studies. *Emotional and Behavioural Difficulties*, 6(2): 69–89.

Foucault, M. (1977) *Discipline and Punish*. NY: Pantheon.

Freire, P. (1970) *Pedagogy of the Oppressed*. London: Routledge.

Furman, W., Rahe, D.F. and Hartup, W.W. (1979) Rehabilitation of Socially Withdrawn Preschool Children through Mixed Age and Same Age Socialisation. *Child Development*, 50(4): 77–89.

Garner, P. (2009) *Special Educational Needs: The Key Concepts*. London: Routledge.

Garrick, R., Bath, C., Dunn, K., Maconochie, H., Willis, B. and Wolstenholme, C. (2010) *Children's Experiences of the Early Years Foundation Stage*. DFE–RB071. London: Department for Education.

Goldschmied, E. and Jackson, S. (1994) *People under Three: Young Children in Day Care*. London: Routledge.

Goldschmied, E. & Jackson, S. (2004) *People Under Three: Young Children in Day Care* (2nd edition). London: Routledge.

Graham, A. (2011) *Early Intervention: The Next Steps – An Independent Report to Her Majesty's Government*. London: HMSO. Available at: www.dwp.gov.uk/docs/early-intervention-next-steps.pdf.

Graham, L.J. and Slee, R. (2008) An Illusory Interiority: Interrogating the Discourse/s of Inclusion. *Educational Philosophy and Theory*, 40(2): 277–93.

Greig, A. and Taylor, J. (1999) *Doing Research with Children*. London: SAGE.

Griffiths, M. (2009) *Action for Social Justice in Education: Fairly Different*. Buckingham: OUP.

Guasp, A. (2011) *Different Families: The Experiences of Children with Lesbian and Gay Parents*. London: Stonewall/Education for All.

Gunner, A. (1997) Children's Rights = Human Rights, *Children UK*, 15(Winter): 12–13.

Gussin Paley, V. (1984) *Boys and Girls: Superheroes in the Doll Corner*. Chicago, IL, and London: University of Chicago Press.

Gussin Paley, V. (1992) *You can't say 'You can't play'*. Chicago and London: University of Chicago Press.

Gussin Paley, V. (1996) Foreword. In L. Koplow (ed.), *Unsmiling Faces: How Preschools Can Heal*. New York: Teachers College Press.

Hall, S. A. (2009) The Social Inclusion of People with Disabilities. A Qualitative Meta-analysis. *Journal of Ethnographic and Qualitative Research*, 2(3): 162–173.

Hannon, P. & Nutbrown, C. (1997) *Preparing for Early Literacy Work with Parents: A Professional Development Manual*. The REAL Project. University of Sheffield.

Harris, N., Eden, K. and Blair, A. (2003) *Challenges to School Exclusion: Exclusion, Appeals and the Law*. London: Routledge Falmer.

Harwood, V. and Rasmussen, M.L. (2002) *Inspiring Methodological Provocateurs in Inclusive Educational Research*. Work in Progress Paper presented at American Educational Research Association.

HMSO (1988) Education Reform Act 1988 London: HMSO.

Holland, P. (1999) Is 'zero-tolerance' intolerance? An under-fives centre takes a fresh look at their policy on war/weapons/superhero practice. *Early Childhood Practice*, 1(1): 24–45.

Holmes, R. (1998) *Fieldwork with Children*. London: Sage.

Hu, B Y., Roberts, S.K., Wang Y. and Zhao H. (2011) The Initiation of Early Childhood Inclusion in China: A Case Study from Beijing. *International Journal of Early Years Education*, DOI:10.1080/09669760.2011.596396.

Hurst. V. and Joseph, J. (1998) *Supporting Early Learning: The Way Forward*. Buckingham: Open University Press.

Hyder, T. (2004) *War, Conflict and Play-Debating Play*. Buckingham: Open University Press.

Jackson, L. (2012) *Securing Standards, Sustaining Success: Report on Early Intervention*. London: National Education Trust.

Jones, P. and Welch, S. (2010) *Rethinking Children's Rights: Attitudes in Contemporary Society*. London: Continuum.

Karran, S. (2003) 'Auntie-Ji, please come and join us, just for an hour.' The role of the bilingual education assistant in working with parents with little confidence. In J. Devereaux and L. Miller (eds), *Working with Children in the Early Years*. London: David Fulton/Open University.

Karsten, S., Peetsma, T., Roeleveld, J. and Vergeer, M. (2001) The Dutch Policy of Integration Put to the Test: Differences in Academic and Psychosocial Development of Pupils in Special and Mainstream Education. *European Journal of Special Needs Education*, 16(3): 193–205.

Katz, L.G. (1995) *Talks with Teachers of Young Children: A Collection*. Norwood, NJ: Ablex.

Kirby, P. and Bryson, S. (2002) *Measuring the Magic? Evaluating and Researching Young People's Participation in Public Decision Making*. Carnegie Young People Initiative: London.

Kress, G.R. (2000) *Literacy in the New Media Age*. London: Routledge Falmer.

Laevers, F. (2002) Forward to Basics! Deep-level-learning and the Experimental Approach. *Early Years*, 20(2): 20–29.

Lancaster, Y. (2003) *Listening to Young Children: Promoting Listening to Young Children: The Reader*. Maidenhead: Open University Press.

Lane, J. (2008) *Young Children and Racial Justice: Taking Action for Racial Equality in the Early Years – Understanding the Past, Thinking about the Present, Planning for the Future*. London: National Children's Bureau (NCB).

Lansdown, G. (1998) The European Convention on Human Rights: Implications for children in the UK. In Children in Scotland 1998: Children's Rights = Human Rights? An examination of Human Rights Standards and their Capacity to Promote and Defend the Rights of Children. Children in Scotland, Edinburgh.

Learning and Teaching Scotland (2010) *Pre-Birth to Three: Positive Outcomes for Scotland's Children and Families*. Scotland: Learning and Teaching Scotland.

Leask, J. (2001) Sam's invisible extra gear – a parent's view. In L. Abbott and C. Nutbrown (eds), *Experiencing Reggio Emilia: Implications for Preschool Provision*. Buckingham: Open University Press.

Leitch, R. and Mitchell, S. (2007) Caged Birds and Cloning Machines: How Student Imagery Speaks to us about Cultures of Schooling and Student Participation. *Improving Schools*, 10(1): 53–71.

Leney, T. (1999) European Approaches to Social Exclusion. In A. Hayton (ed.), *Tackling Disaffection and Social Exclusion: Education Perspectives and Policies*. Kogan Page: London.

Leslie, R. (2005) Seeing gender through young girls' eyes. In K. Hirst and C. Nutbrown (eds), *Perspectives on Early Childhood Education: Essays in Contemporary Research*. Stoke-on-Trent: Trentham Books.

Lewis, A. and Lindsay, G. (eds) *Researching Children's Perspectives*. Buckingham: Open University Press.

Levitas, R. (1998) *The Inclusive Society? Social Exclusion and New Labour*. Basingstoke: Macmillan.

Lindon, J. (2001) *Understanding Children's Play*. Cheltenham: Nelson Thornes.

Lingard, B. (2000) Profile: Bob Lingard. In P. Clough and J. Corbett, *Theories of Inclusive Education*. London: Paul Chapman Publishers/Sage.

Lipsky, D.K. and Gartner, A. (1996) Inclusion, School Restructuring and the Remaking of American Society. *Harvard Educational Review*, 66(4): 762–96.

Lowenfeld, M. (1935) *Play in Childhood*. London: Gollancz.

Maccoby, E.E. and Jacklin, C.N. (1974) *The Psychology of Sex Differences* (Vol. 1). Stanford, CA: Stanford University Press.

MacNaughton, G. (1999) Even pink tents have glass ceilings: crossing the gender boundaries in pretend play. In E. Dau, E. and E. Jones (eds), *Child's Play: Revisiting Play in Early Childhood Settings*. Sydney: MacLennan and Petty.

MacNaughton, G. (2000) *Rethinking Gender in Early Childhood Education*. London: Sage.

MacNaughton, G., Hughes, P. and Smith, K. (2007) Young Children's Rights and Public Policy: Practices and Possibilities for Citizenship in the Early Years. *Children & Society*, 21(6): 458–469.

Malaguzzi, L. (1995) A charter of rights. In *A Journey into the Rights of Children: As Seen by the Children Themselves* (pp. 67–69). Reggio Emilia: Reggio Children.

Malaguzzi, L. (1996) The right to environment. In T. Filippini and V. Vecchi (eds), *The Hundred Languages of Children: The Exhibit*. Reggio Emilia: Reggio Children.

Malaguzzi, L. (1998) History, ideas and basic philosophy: an interview with Lella Gandini. In C. Edwards, L. Gandini and G. Foreman (1998). *The Hundred Languages of Children: The Reggio Emilia Approach – Advanced Reflections* (2nd edition). Westport, CT: Ablex Publishing.

Manning, K. and Sharp, A. (1977) *Structuring Play in the Early Years at School*. London: Ward Lock Educational.

Manning-Morton, J. and Thorp, M. (2004) *Key Times for Play*. Buckingham: Open University Press.

Marsh, J. and Thompson, P. (2001) Parental Involvement in Literacy Development: Using Media Texts. *Journal of Research in Reading* 24(3): 266–78.

Matthews, M. (1994) *Science Teaching: The Role of History and Philosophy of Science*. New York: Routledge.

Mauthner, M. (1997) Methodological Aspects of Collecting Data from Children: Lessons from Three Research Projects. *Children and Society*, 11(1): 16–28.

McDonald, A.P., Brownell, K. and Worley, M. (1997) Teaching experience and specialist support: a survey of preschool teachers employed in programs accredited by Miedzian, M. (1992) *Boys will be Boys*. London: Virago Press.

Meijer, C.J.W. (1998) *Integration in Europe: Provision for Pupils with Special Educational Needs. Trends in 14 European Countries*. European Agency for Developments in Special Needs Education. Denmark: Middelfart.

Miedzian, M. (1992) *Boys will be Boys: Breaking the Link Between Masculinity and Violence*. London: Virago.

Milner, D. (1983) *Children and Race: Ten Years On*. London: Ward Lock.

Moons, J. and Kog, M. (1997) *A Box Full of Feelings* (manual), Centre for Experiential Education, University of Leuven.

Mosely, J. (2001) *Here We Go Round: Quality Circle Time for 3–5 Year Olds*. Trowbridge: Positive Press.

NAEYC (National Association for the Education of the Young Child) (1996). Available at: www.naeyc.org

NAW (National Assembly for Wales) (2003) *The Learning Country: The Foundation Phase – 3 to 7 Years*. Cardiff: National Assembly for Wales.

New Zealand Ministry of Education (1995) *Te Whariki: Early Childhood Curriculum*. Wellington: Learning Media.

Nurse, A. (2001) A question of inclusion. In L. Abbott and C. Nutbrown (eds), *Experiencing Reggio Emilia: Implication for Preschool Education*. Buckingham: Open University Press.

Nutbrown, C. (ed.) (1996) *Respectful Educators – Capable Learners: Children's Rights and Early Education*. London: Paul Chapman Publishers/Sage.

Nutbrown, C. (1998) Managing to include? Rights, responsibilities and respect. In P. Clough (ed.), *Managing Inclusive Education: From Policy and Experience*. London: Paul Chapman Publishers/Sage.

Nutbrown, C. (ed.) (2002a) *Research Studies in Early Childhood Education*. Stoke-on-Trent: Trentham Books.

Nutbrown, C. (2002b) Early childhood education in contexts of change. In C. Nutbrown (ed.), *Research Studies in Early Childhood Education*. Stoke-on-Trent: Trentham Books.

Nutbrown, C. (2010) *Key Concepts in Early Education and Care*. London: Sage.

Nutbrown, C. (2011) *Threads of Thinking: Schemas and Young Children Learning* (4th edition). London: Sage.

Nutbrown, C. (2012) *Foundations for Quality: The Independent Review of Early Education and Childcare Qualifications Final Report*. London: Department for Education.

Nutbrown, C. and Clough, P. (2003) *Inclusion and Exclusion: Perspectives from European Early Childhood Educators*. Paper presented at the European Early Childhood Education Research Association Conference, University of Strathclyde, September.

Nutbrown, C. and Clough, P. (2004) Inclusion in the early years: conversations with european educators. *European Journal of Special Needs Education*, 19(3): 311–39.

Nutbrown, C. and Clough, P. (2009) Citizenship and inclusion in the early years: understanding and responding to children's perspectives on 'belonging'. *International Journal of Early Years Education*, 17(3): 191–205.

Nutbrown, C. and Drummond, M.J. (1996) Observing and assessing young children. In G. Pugh (ed.), *Contemporary Issues in the Early Years: Working Collaboratively for Children* (2nd edition). London: Paul Chapman Publishing.

Nutbrown, C. and Hannon, P. (eds) (1997) *Preparing for Early Literacy Work with Families: A Professional Development Manual*. Nottingham/Sheffield: NES Arnold/REAL Project.

Nutbrown, C., Hannon, P. and Morgan, A. (2005) *Early Literacy Work with Parents: Policy, Practice and Research*. London: Sage.

Nutbrown, C. and Page, J. (2008) *Working with Babies and Young Children from Birth to Three*. London: Sage.

OECD (2001) *Starting Strong: Early Childhood Education and Care*. Paris: Organisation for Economic Cooperation and Development.

Parker, C. (2002) Working with families on curriculum: developing shared understandings of children's mark making. In C. Nutbrown (ed.), *Research Studies in Early Childhood Education*. Stoke-on-Trent: Trentham Books.

Papatheodorou, T. (2002) How we like our schools to be … pupils' voices. *European Educational Research Journal*, 1(3): 445–467.

Penn, H. (1999) How should we care for babies and toddlers? An analysis of practice in out-of-home settings for children under three. Occasional Paper 10.6.1999 iv (66pp). Childcare Resource and Research Unit, University of Toronto, Canada.

Perera, S. (2001) Living with 'Special Educational Needs': mothers' perspectives. In P. Clough and C. Nutbrown (eds), *Voices of Arabia: Essays in Educational Research*. University of Sheffield Papers in Education. Sheffield: University of Sheffield.

Phillips, S. (2001) Special needs or special rights? In L. Abbott and C. Nutbrown (eds), *Experiencing Reggio Emilia: Implication for Preschool Education*. Buckingham: Open University Press.

Popkewitz, T. and Lindblad, S. (2000) Educational governance and social inclusion and exclusion: some conceptual difficulties and problematics in policy and research. *Discourse: Studies in the Cultural Politics of Education*, 21(1): 5–44.

Poulou, M. and Norwich, B. (2000) Teachers' perceptions of students with emotional and behavioural difficulties: severity and prevalence. *European Journal of Special Needs Education*, 15(2): 171–87.

Powell, J. (2005) Anti-discriminatory practice matters. In L. Abbot and A. Langston (eds), *Birth to Three Matters: Supporting the Framework of Effective Practice*. Maidenhead: Open University Press.

Pugh, G. and Selleck, D.R. (1996) Listening to and communicating with young children. In R. Davie, G. Upton and V. Varma (eds), *The Voice of the Child, A Handbook for Professionals*. London: Falmer.

QCA/DfES (2008a) *Curriculum Guidance for the Foundation Stage*. London: Qualifications and Curriculum Authority/Department for Education and Skills.

QCA/DfES (2008b) *Foundation Stage Profile Handbook*. London: Qualifications and Curriculum Authority/Department for Education and Skills.

QCAAW (Qualifications Curriculum and Assessment Authority for Wales) (2004) *The Foundation Phase in Wales: A Draft Framework for Children's Learning*. Cardiff: National Assembly for Wales.

Rinaldi, C. (1999) *The Pedagogy of Listening*. Paper given at the Reggio Emilia Conference, Reggio Emilia, Italy, 28 April.

Rinaldi, C. (2005) *In Dialogue with Reggio Emilia: Contextualising, Interpreting and Evaluating Early Childhood Education*. London: Routledge.

Roberts, R. (2006) *Self-esteem and Early Learning* (3rd edition). London: Hodder and Stoughton.

Rogoff, B. (1990) *Apprenticeship in Thinking: Cognitive Development in Social Context*. Oxford: Oxford University Press.

Rogow, S. (1991) The dynamics of play: including children with special needs in mainstreamed early childhood programmes. *International Journal of Early Childhood*, 23(2): 50–7.

Said, E.W. (1978) *Orientalism*. New York: Pantheon.

Sandberg, A. and Heden, R. (2011) Play's importance in school. *Education*, 3(13): 317–29.

SCAA (School Curriculum and Assessment Authority) (1996) *Desirable Outcomes for Nursery Education*. London: SCAA.

SCAA (School Curriculum and Assessment Authority) (1997) *National Framework for Baseline Assessment: Criteria and Procedures for the Accreditation of Baseline Assessment Schemes*. London: SCAA.

Schweinhart, L.J., Barnes, H.V. and Weikart, D.P. (1993) *Significant Benefits: The High Scope Perry Preschool Study through age 27*, Monograph of the High Scope Educational Research Foundation, 10. Ypsilanti, MI: High Scope Press.

Schweinhart, L.J., Montie, J., Xiang, Z., Barnett, W.S., Belfield, C.R. and Nores, M. (2004) *Lifetime Effects: The High Scope Perry Preschool Study through age 40*, Monographs of the High Scope Educational Research Foundation. Ypsilanti, MI: High Scope Press.

Scottish Consultative Council on the Curriculum (1999) *Curriculum Framework for Children 3 to 5*. Dundee: Scottish Consultative Council on the Curriculum.

Scottish Executive (2003) *Integrated Strategy for Early Years* (Consultation Document). Edinburgh: Children and Young People's Group/Scottish Executive.

Scottish Government (2008) *Curriculum for Excellence: Building the Curriculum 3. A Framework for Learning and Teaching*. Edinburgh: Scottish Government.

Scruggs, T.E. and Mastropieri, M.A. (1996) Teacher perceptions of mainstreaming inclusion 1958–1995: a research synthesis. *Exceptional Children*, 63(1): 59–74.

Selleck, D. and Griffin, S. (1996) Quality for the under threes. In G. Pugh (ed.), *Contemporary Issues in the Early Years: Working Collaboratively for Children* (2nd edition). London: Paul Chapman Publishing.

Shotton, J. (1998) *Learning and Freedom*. New Delhi: Sage.

Singer, E. and Hännikainen, M. (2002) The Teacher's Role in Territorial Conflicts of 2- to 3-year-old Children. *Journal of Research in Childhood Education*, 17: 5–18.

Siraj-Blatchford, I. (1994) *Early Years – Laying the Foundations for Racial Equality*. Nottingham: Trentham Books.

Sparkes, A.C. (1999) Exploring Body Narratives. *Sport Education and Society*, 4(1): 17–30.

Stonewall (2010) *Including Different Families*. London: Stonewall/Education for All.

Swadener, B.B., Grant, C.A., Mitakidou, S. and Tressou, E. (2009) *Beyond Pedagogies of Exclusion in Diverse Childhood Contexts: Transnational Challenges* (Critical Cultural Studies of Childhood). New York: Palgrave Macmillan.

Tacey, C. (2005) Why do boys like to build and girls like to draw? Gender issues in a small British military community. In K. Hirst and C. Nutbrown (eds), *Perspectives on Early Childhood Education: Essays in Contemporary Research*. Stoke-on-Trent: Trentham Books.

Tarullo, L.B. (1994) Windows on social worlds: gender differences in children's play – narratives. In A. Slade and P.D. Wolf (eds), *Children at Play: Clinical and Developmental Approaches to Meaning and Representation*. New York: Oxford University Press.

Tickell, C. (2011) *Review of the Early Years Foundation Stage*. London: DfE.

UNESCO (1992) United Nations Convention on the Rights of the Child. Paris: UNESCO.

UNESCO (1994) *The Salamanca Statement and Framework for Action on Special Needs Education*. Paris: UNESCO.

UNESCO Dakar Framework for Action 2000

UNESCO (2000) *Education for All in the Americas: Regional Framework of Action*. Paris: UNESCO. Available at: www.unesco.org/education/efa/wef_2000/regional_frameworks/fram_americas.shtml.

UNICEF (2011) *Pocket Book of Children's Rights*. New York: UNICEF. Available at: https://unicef.org.uk/Education/ResourcesOverview/Resources/Pocket-Book-of-Childrens-Rights/.

United Nations (1989) *Convention on the Rights of the Child*. New York: UN.

Vakil, S., Freeman, R. and Swim, T.J. (2003) The Reggio Emilia Approach and Inclusive Early Childhood Programmes. *Early Childhood Education Journal*, 30(3): 187–192, 210.

Valentine, K. (2009) Accounting for Agency. *Children & Society* 25(5): 347–358, DOI: 10.1111/j.1099-0860.2009.00279.x

Valentine, M. (1999) *The Reggio Emilia Approach to Early Years Education*. Dundee: Scottish Consultative Council on the Curriculum.

Visser, J., Cole, T. and Daniels, H. (2003) Inclusion for the difficult to include. In M. Nind, K. Sheehy and K. Simmons (eds), *Inclusive Education: Learners and Learning Contexts*. London: David Fulton.

Vygotsky, L.S. (1978) *Mind in Society* Cambridge: MA Harvard University Press.

WAG (Welsh Assembly Government) (2008) *Framework for Children's Learning for 3- to 7-year-olds in Wales*. Cardiff: WAG.

Waldon, N.L. and McLeskey, J. (1998) The effects of an inclusive education program on students with mild and severe learning disabilities. *Exceptional Children*, 64(3): 395–405.

Wall, K. (2010) *Special Needs and Early Years: A Practitioner Guide*. London: Sage.

Walters, N. (2002) Gender roles and toys in the home: parents' attitudes and children's experiences. In C. Nutbrown (ed.), *Research Studies in Early Childhood Education*. Stoke-on Trent: Trentham.

Wedge, P. and Prosser, H. (1973) Born to fail? *National Children's Bureau/Arrow Books*, 20(7): 1–64.

Weinberger, J., Pickstone, C. and Hannon, P. (eds) (2005) *Learning from Sure Start*. London: Routledge Falmer.

Welsh Assembly Government (2008) *Framework for Children's Learning for 3 to 7 year-olds in Wales*. Cardiff: WAG.

Whalley, M. and the Pen Green Centre Team (1997) *Involving Parents in Their Children's Learning*. London: Paul Chapman Publishing.

Wheeler, H. (2009) *Parents, Early Years and Learning: Parents as Partners in the Early Years Foundation Stage*. London: National Children's Bureau.

Whitehurst, G.J., Epstein, J.N., Angell, A.L., Payne, D.A., Crone, D.A. and Fischel, J.E. (1994) Outcomes of an Emergent Literacy Intervention in Head Start. *Journal of Educational Psychology*, 86(4): 542–55.

Wolfendale, S. (ed.) (2000) *Special Needs in the Early Years: Snapshots of Practice*. London: Routledge Falmer.

Zigmond, N. and Baker, J.M. (1996) Full inclusion for students with learning disabilities: too much of a good thing? *Theory into Practice*, 35(1): 26–34.

Author Index

Subject Index